D0070100

WHY SOLDIERS MISS WAR

WHY SOLDIERS MISS WAR

MISS WAR

The Journey Home

NOLAN PETERSON

CASEMATE

Philadelphia & Oxford

ST. JOHN THE BAPTIST PARISH LIBRARY
2920 NEW HIGHWAY 51
LAPLACE, LOUISIANA 70068

Published in the United States of America and Great Britain in 2019 by
CASEMATE PUBLISHERS
1950 Lawrence Road, Havertown, PA 19083, USA
and
The Old Music Hall, 106–108 Cowley Road, Oxford OX4 1JE, UK

Copyright 2019 © Nolan Peterson

Hardcover Edition: ISBN 978-1-61200-773-1
Digital Edition: ISBN 978-1-61200-774-8

A CIP record for this book is available from the British Library

All rights reserved. No part of this book may be reproduced or transmitted in any form
or by any means, electronic or mechanical including photocopying, recording or by any
information storage and retrieval system, without permission from the publisher in writing.

Printed and bound in the United States of America

Typeset in India for Casemate Publishing Services. www.casematepublishingservices.com

For a complete list of Casemate titles, please contact:

CASEMATE PUBLISHERS (US)
Telephone (610) 853-9131
Fax (610) 853-9146
Email: casemate@casematepublishers.com
www.casematepublishers.com

CASEMATE PUBLISHERS (UK)
Telephone (01865) 241249
Email: casemate-uk@casematepublishers.co.uk
www.casematepublishers.co.uk

Front cover: While U.S. warplanes roar overhead, Kurdish peshmerga soldiers at a front-line
fort near Mosul look across no man's land toward ISIS positions.
All images from author's collection.

"In the fall the war was always there, but we did not go to it anymore."

ERNEST HEMINGWAY

For Mom and Dad

*You gave me
wings, and I flew
my way home.*

Contents

Foreword

Why do young men and women join the military? And when they do join, and are asked to fight, what is it about combat that keeps pulling them back?

As strange as it seems, in 1971 as a high school senior I had the desire to fight for my country in a faraway land where very few others wanted to go. The desire to fight a war that was tearing our nation apart was unusual during that period that was unique in our history. Even while others were dodging the draft and finding ways to avoid the conscript force that existed at the time, I wanted to join the Army. But it wasn't all selfless service for me... while serving our nation and having a vision of a life filled with adventure and travel away from a city I had never left in my first 18 years of life were the primary reasons I wanted to wear the cloth of the country, serving also came with the opportunity to get a free college education neither my lower-income family nor I could afford. After passing the academic requirements and garnering a senator's appointment that very few others wanted during the Vietnam era, I boarded an airplane for the first time and traveled from Missouri to New York City. It was the first leg of my journey to West Point, and the start of a life as a soldier.

But here's the interesting part about my volunteering for Vietnam by first submitting myself to the spartan environment of West Point while most of my friends were going to civilian colleges. From the day I entered the US Military Academy in July of 1971 to the time

I graduated in June of 1975, things changed. While almost all of our active duty Army professors that were cycling through duty at West Point were telling their stories of leading troops in Vietnam and the dynamics of the Southeast Asian conflict that they wanted each of us impressionable and potential new officers to learn about before joining them on the field of battle, by the end of our sophomore year it was obvious that none of us would ever see action in that particular war. No member of my class of 1975 would ever serve in the fight that was raging when we entered West Point, wide-eyed, innocent, and itching for a fight.

For us, the "Cold War" classes of the late 1970s and early 1980s prepared us instead for the Warsaw Pact or the North Korean and Chinese hordes. We didn't see action until much later in our careers, when we were sent to Grenada, Panama and Operation *Desert Storm*.

Operation *Desert Storm* was my first combat deployment, and it came to me when I was a major, serving in Germany. Up until the time we were told to deploy to the desert of the Middle East, our Army had just begun experiencing the peace dividend that was a result of the inter-German Wall coming down, and I was 15 years into an Army career before ever firing a shot in anger. In fact, a month before we were notified by the secretary of defense via a press conference broadcasted on Armed Forces Network that our 1st Armored Division Cavalry Squadron would deploy, I distinctly remember sitting in a German *Gasthaus* with a fellow major drinking a Hefeweizen discussing how we would likely be the first class of West Point graduates who would never see conflict. Two months later, we were rehearsing offensive operations in the Saudi Arabian desert, preparing to cross the berm into southern Iraq. We were finally preparing for what we had signed up to do.

Four short days—100 hours of battle that followed a month of aerial bombardment of our Iraqi foes—was my first taste of combat operations. During those 89 hours, I was involved in several skirmishes, had taken the lives of Iraqi conscripts and some members of the vaunted Iraqi Republican Guard, and was wounded in action. Then it was over.

Most Americans believe that war was fought against mostly beaten Iraqi soldiers who surrendered to the juggernaut of an expertly led and brilliantly executed conventional ground campaign. But at the tactical level, there were plenty of fights. Our cavalry squadron was predicted to sustain 50 percent casualties (we actually had 31 wounded in action, none killed), and we experienced some intense and devastating fighting (to include conducting a forward passage of lines through our advance guard of the armored brigade that would be engaged in the largest tank battle since Kursk in World War II). On one occasion, at close range, I shot an Iraqi soldier in the chest with a .45 pistol. When he fell forward and his helmet fell off his head to the ground, I saw a photograph of his wife and two children inside the liner. Tankers like me are trained to kill the enemy at long range, so that intimate killing event is a memory that continues to haunt me.

All soldiers lose a large part of their innocence in combat. Whether you're an 18-year-old infantryman, a 22-year-old pilot dropping bombs, or a 35-year-old major, killing another living being has an emotional and psychological effect. The day I shot that Iraqi soldier in a trench in southern Iraq was the day I lost my innocence.

Returning home a few months later I didn't tell anyone about any of this, nor did I tell them about the artillery barrage our cavalry unit was subjected to… likely a case of friendly fire, though it was never proven. But at a Long Island Fourth of July celebration the summer after we returned, I had the first of what would be many strange delayed emotional reactions when the overhead fireworks were a little too reminiscent of combat. That was the start of a period of time when I lost a bit more of my psychological equilibrium, suffering from what Canadian and British veterans returning from the trenches of World War I called "a soldier's heart." A melancholy, extended self-reflection and a search for meaning is associated with that malady then and now, but today all those factors are associated with post-traumatic stress. Lucky for me, I had a spouse who helped me face my demons, and her understanding and counseling allowed me to regain the lost resilience. The recovery and greater understanding came in pretty handy when I faced two more combat tours, each lasting 15 months in an environment that was much more intense than *Desert Storm*.

I'm thankful for all of those experiences. I know what I went through contributed to a better understanding of what the other soldiers I commanded later in my career experienced, since each of them eventually would encounter their own demons when the sights and sounds of war affected their lives.

Since I've retired, civilians who have not had military service have asked me to tell them stories about Cold War adventures, deployments and assignments around the globe, stressful multinational engagements, or the terrific people with whom I've served. I willingly talk about those things. In most cases, I relate a few anecdotes because—depending on the situation—stories about a career soldier's exploits and travels are known to evoke laughter, tears, a gamut of emotions: major mistakes, minor successes, tales of short and long times away from home, dangers, awe, and hardships. The stories will likely also have undercurrents of family, shared values, memories of comrades, and also indications of extensive time spent in reflection... and attempts at growth and self-healing.

But stories about combat experiences are different, and the many accounts I could tell about the three-plus years of combat I've experienced are not those I share with just anyone. When any veterans recount the narratives of their combat experience, no matter the conflict, unexpected reactions will often bubble up from the memories that are seared into the description, the anecdotes, the events. And usually, combat veterans will not share those descriptions with those who have not had similar experiences. Once, while I was commanding the US Army in Europe and had the chance to attend a Normandy commemoration in St Mère Eglise, France, I was given the honor of engaging with a group of 90-plus-year-old World War II veterans who had landed on the beaches or flown bombers and fighters overhead. As the beer flowed, they told me—because I was a fellow combat veteran, albeit from a different war—some of their experiences. These older gentlemen openly shared their stories and their emotions, in hushed tones and deeply moving and pained accounts. A young woman in the back who was straining to hear her grandfather-veteran unleash his memories approached me in tears after the evening. She related she always thought she had an extremely close relationship with her "pops," and that was the reason she wanted to come with him to this commemoration. But then she added, through uncontrollable tears, that she had never heard any of his somber and human stories about the war, and she had never seen him cry before. She had never known that side of him.

Another time, while discussing the intricacies of medical healthcare with a military trauma physician who had spent multiple deployments to different theaters treating soldiers in Somalia, Iraq, and Afghanistan, I asked how he dealt with all his memories of carnage and torn bodies. He stared at me, and then he spoke quietly so I could just hear him. "I cry at unexpected times," he said. "I can't explain it, but sometimes all the memories just become too overwhelming. I really can't put a finger on what specific things cause me to start sobbing, but I think it's because I am still trying to figure out the loss of young people."

Not all combat veterans suffer from PTS, and a smaller percentage are assessed to have true PTSD. But everyone that has experienced combat has lost their innocence. As a commander, and as a father of two soldiers who have deployed multiple times, I have seen this first hand. Whether the wars we send our young people to are just and honorable, or ill-considered and immoral, the vast majority of those who fight return with a desire to regain normalcy, life's simplicity, their soul's virtue—their innocence. Few of them are completely successful in doing so.

Nolan Peterson is a veteran of combat, a war correspondent, and a journalistic observer of conflicts that are being waged in multiple cultures. He and I are of different generations, but like many of his fellow millennials he faced combat upon entering the service at a young age. He and all the others of his ilk were thrown into a cauldron of repeated deployments with continuous stress in today's combat—a cacophony of sights, sounds, smells, tastes, and tactile feelings. His battles were unremitting, uninterrupted and a repeated assault on the senses that cannot be replicated in any artificial or simulated environment. The mixture of fear, fatigue, passion and movement batters the muscles, hormones, and neurological pathways. The environment and the requirements of combat ravage every individual who experiences it, and Nolan has seen it all.

When Nolan asked me to read the first draft of his book, I was surprised (shocked?) by the request—and by the title. What kind of a story is he going to tell, and does he really have some universal truth that might also provide me with the answer as to why—though this is something I will never tell anyone—there is something in all of us who can't figure out, or who miss, our experiences in war? After all, though I retired with a higher rank, Nolan certainly has more encounters than me, given he served in Afghanistan and Iraq and went back to report on conflicts in both those countries, as well as—and most especially—a very unique and ongoing war inflicted by Russia in Ukraine. He has seen insurgencies, conventional fights, terrorism, irredentism, genocides, and many other types of conflicts, as well as examined many more cultures where people are fighting for freedoms. He must have figured something out.

Here's a spoiler alert: He has figured something out, and I've come to learn that we're not different at all. We see things the same way. We've both faced the inner turmoil, punished ourselves through hours of self-reflection, tackled the demons that often come out of nowhere to haunt us, attempted to determine how so many emotions and values—compassion, humility, integrity, trust, selflessness, courage, empathy, dignity—all come together in places where human tragedy and dysfunction coexist.

This book will be devoured by those who have experienced war, and who are still trying to figure out war's meaning and war's effect on their lives. This book will also provide insight for those who have never experienced war, but who want to know about the sacrifices that are shouldered by a small number of our fellow citizens who wear the uniform and who serve our nation. Finally, this book offers a valuable and moving insight into what it's like to physically come back from war—and how, as life goes on, war always retains its place in our minds, hearts, and souls, until it is replaced and shoved aside by something more important.

General Mark Hertling
July 2019

Prologue

A layer of fine brown dust hung in the air. Out in the distance, snow-capped mountains formed a jagged horizon while C-130 transport planes and Apache helicopter gunships roared overhead like an irregular heartbeat to the unseen war beyond the wire.

"You wanna see where the rocket landed?" Sgt. 1st Class Jeffrey Martin asked me.

"Yeah, of course," I replied.

Martin parked the Toyota Hilux truck outside the US Army tactical operations center's defensive perimeter of concrete slabs. He hesitated before getting out.

Knowing what was in store for me later on, Martin asked, "How you doing?"

"I'm fine," I replied automatically, not knowing if it was a lie. "I'm sure it'll sink in later."

The soldier said nothing.

It was December 2013 and I was embedded with the US Army in eastern Afghanistan as a foreign correspondent for United Press International. On this day we were at FOB Shank, a joint US-Afghan forward operating base in Logar Province. Hills and urban areas dotted the dusty valley around the base, offering plenty of places for Taliban militants to hide and lob one-off rocket and mortar shots. In fact, due to the frequency of Taliban attacks US soldiers jokingly referred to FOB Shank as "Rocket City." Consequently, the place was constructed like a medieval castle. Reinforced concrete and rebar bunkers lined with sandbags and stocked with first-aid kits were never more than sprinting distance away. When the air-raid alarm went off, as it did several times a day, you had two choices.

If you weren't near a bunker you just dropped to the ground, covered your head with your arms and prayed silently that the incoming round didn't hit anywhere near you. You kept your eyes down and stared at something close, like a seam on the plywood floor of the room you were in, or at a pebble or blade of grass in the field where you lay. You focused on that nearby vision and on the sound of the alarm and waited for evidence of the exploding Taliban weapon, hoping that it was a distant thud and not a flash of red and white and then heat and then darkness. Survival was reduced to a few seconds of waiting and pure luck.

If you happened to be near a bunker, then you got your butt under cover. The entrances to the bunkers were open to the outside with another vertical concrete slab a few yards away, ostensibly to block horizontal shrapnel. You could usually see blue sky out the entrance, though, which always made me wonder what would happen if a well-placed mortar found its way into that little unprotected, open space. Such a scenario would turn the bunker into a death trap. But the odds of that happening were low. And survival was all about the odds. There's something simultaneously comforting and terrifying about that truth, once you understand it.

Martin and I left the truck and walked across the gravel clearing beyond the fortress walls of the US Army compound. It was mid afternoon, and we had just eaten lunch. A standard chow hall meal of some indescribable meat and soggy vegetables, topped off with a few Rip-Its for a caffeine kick.

"Jesus," Martin said as we looked at the charred crater where the Taliban rocket had impacted. "We're so fucking lucky to be alive."

As if on cue, we both looked up and in the direction of the rocket's flight path. Along that vector was a radio antenna within the Army compound. A few hours prior, Martin and I had been standing near its base, chatting while we sipped on Blue Monster energy drinks. (Caffeine was a staple of deployed life.) When the attack came, we survived by diving into a concrete bunker that, as luck would have it, was only a few feet away. In the distance behind the antenna, slightly obscured in the valley's eternal brown haze and well beyond the base perimeter, was a low bluff covered in typically drab Afghan buildings. At that moment, Apache gunships patrolled the skies above this distant area.

"That must be where the fucker shot from," Martin said. "Although they always put the rockets on timers and run away before they shoot. Don't know why they're still looking for him. He's long gone."

Martin estimated the Taliban militant had aimed the rocket at the tower since it was an easily identifiable landmark at a distance. It had been a good shot, Martin remarked. The rocket might have impacted the tower had the Phalanx Close-In Weapons System not shot it down.

"We killed off most of the experienced Taliban fighters long ago," Martin said. "That one obviously had pretty good aim, so he's probably been around a while. It also means he knows how to disappear."

* * *

Earlier, Martin's eyes had opened wide at the sound of the incoming alarm. He had spun and instinctively moved to the bunker before it even registered in my mind what was happening. I hesitated, my instincts not as finely tuned or ingrained as his.

There was the thud of an explosion followed by the sound of the Phalanx guns firing. Then the shifting pitch of shrapnel flying past, similar to quickly running your fingernail down tightly stretched nylon—*phhh-thew, phhh-thew, phhh-thew*...

I made it inside the bunker behind Martin by a couple yards. We stood there with both our chests heaving and I could feel my heart beating like it wanted to leap out of my body. I was unexplainably full of energy, ready to explode.

I started to laugh.

"Holy fuck," Martin said. "Holy fuck, holy fuck, holy fuck."

I scanned my body for injuries, realizing adrenaline had turned me numb. I looked at my hands. Amazingly, I was still holding the Blue Monster can in my right hand, although it had spilled all over my sleeve and pant leg in the dash to the bunker. My adrenaline-enhanced grip had crumpled the aluminum.

My left hand had a deep cut and was bleeding so much the blood dripped on my boots. Apparently, I had scraped it on the wall of the bunker as I scrambled in. I wouldn't have known I was cut, however, if I hadn't seen the wound. I didn't feel a thing.

"We almost had our fucking heads blown off," Martin said, shaking his head, speaking excitedly. "That sound... man, that sounded close."

It felt like we were sharing a joke, or sitting in the stands watching our home team win a game. We were amped up from the adrenaline, just beginning to realize that we had cheated death, overwhelmed by the desire to talk about it, laugh about it, whatever—we just had to share it.

At length other soldiers streamed into the bunker, all smiling and joking. We sat together on two long wooden benches, waiting for the all-clear signal. Everyone wanted to talk, like we were rehearsing our memories for later.

"That was close," one soldier said.

"It blew up right over us," Martin chimed in. He leaned forward with his elbows on his knees, shaking his head as he spoke. "We should be dead."

"How's that for a fucking story?" Martin said, turned to me now. "Wouldn't do you much good to get your head blown off, though. Imagine how much shit I'd be in if I had to explain to my boss how I got a reporter killed."

* * *

After the attack we inspected the exterior of the bunker and found it pockmarked by nickel- and dime-sized shrapnel holes. Any one of those high-velocity, molten metal bits would have been lethal. It was a miracle that Martin and I were alive. The lone Taliban missile fired at FOB Shank had been shot out of the sky about 30 feet over our heads by the Phalanx guns defending the base. The remaining bulk of the missile impacted the ground just beyond the camp's walls, leaving a three-foot-wide crater in the gravel.

The Phalanx system was designed to defend Navy ships from long-range missile attacks, but it had become a staple at US bases in Afghanistan and Iraq, too. Its sophisticated radar and guns could detect enemy rockets and mortars and destroy them midair. The reason Martin and I were so lucky to be alive is that when the Phalanx guns shoot down an enemy projectile, superheated shrapnel—and in the case of the rocket that day, the white phosphorus inside its warhead—typically rain down around the point of impact.

Looking at the bunker's pockmarked walls it seemed almost as if the shrapnel scars had silhouetted our bodies' outlines like in some Roadrunner cartoon. How had we not been hit?

"It's all fun and games until your right testicle is coming out your left nostril and there's a rocket up your ass," Martin told me a little while later. A gloomier attitude had replaced his earlier jubilance at being alive. He wore that thousand-yard stare I had only seen in photographs or movies about war.

"How does it feel to almost get your head blown off?" he inquired.

The truth is, I didn't know. One moment, I found the whole thing pretty hilarious. The next, I was scared.

Reality only truly slithered its way into my thoughts later that evening as Martin drove me back to my room after our detour to visit the crater.

"You okay?" he asked as we went down the dusty perimeter road. The setting sun over the far-off mountains looked particularly beautiful that night. The dust permanently suspended in the Afghan air does make for some incredible sunsets, I must admit.

"Yeah, man. I'm cool. Just crazy, you know?" I said, staring out the window.

We sat in silence until Martin said at last, "You better write home tonight to your family and tell them you love them."

Huh?

I'll just come right out and say this—Martin was not a real sentimental guy. Every other word out of his mouth had four letters. He was a battle-hardened warrior who effortlessly transitioned from talking about the carnage of combat in Baghdad to what was on the menu at the chow hall for dinner, without changing the tone of his voice. The day before, as we ate lunch, he had told me about the 2003 invasion of Iraq.

"We killed about 400 that first night. Just fucking murdered them," he said evenly. "The next morning all their wives and mothers were out looking through the bodies, trying to find their dead men. And man, let me tell you, the place was just covered in dead dudes. We just walked right through them all, those crying women and the dead. They never said anything, though, they didn't even look at us."

He paused for a moment, returning for an instant to some time and place that I could never imagine, and his words could never recreate.

He said, "We killed a lot of dudes."

Well, now, driving his car through the Afghan mountains, this warrior was shaken. But, before I go on, let me define the word "shaken" in this context because I know Martin will read this, and he'll want to kick my ass if I imply that he was scared like I was.

By shaken I mean that Martin knew—much better than some ground-combat novice like myself—just how seriously close we had come to dying. He knew this because he had personally seen a lot of people die. Martin said something to me about how lucky he was to have experienced so much combat without suffering a scratch, despite the countless lives and limbs he had seen torn from his friends and comrades over the years. He was "shaken" because he actually knew what that shrapnel would have done to our bodies. It wasn't a hypothesis like it was for me. He had mental images of that kind of carnage.

"You just can't think about that stuff, though," Martin told me. "It'll make you crazy."

We sat in silence, thinking about the things we shouldn't.

"That sound," Martin finally said, interrupting our solitary thoughts.

"I know that sound." After a moment, he added, "That was close. Too close."

He was talking about the sound of passing bullets or shrapnel. It's a distinctive sound, which, once you've heard it in the context of combat, will always trigger the primal, reptilian part of your brain that guides reflexive life-and-death responses. That's probably why Martin beat me inside the bunker that morning by several seconds. As a veteran of two wars and eight combat deployments, he had been under fire a lot more than me.

"When the bullets are flying and shit starts blowing up, you're not thinking about any of that duty, honor, country bullshit," Martin elaborated. "You focus on taking care of your buddy next to you and making it out alive."

They say that when you're faced with a life-or-death situation your training kicks in and you don't think about what you're doing any more. It's all muscle memory. You just operate on autopilot. That's true, to a degree. Training, after all, is just a safely repeatable substitute for near-death experiences.

In his book, *Outliers*, journalist Malcolm Gladwell makes the case that becoming an expert at a skill requires 10,000 hours of practice. Perhaps that's true. But one near-death experience has a similar effect to those 10,000 hours, ingraining in your memory every action, no matter how minute, that kept you alive. And when any portion of that near-death experience is recreated—the sound of an air-raid alert, a car backfiring, the Doppler shift of the sound of passing shrapnel—the unthinking responses that had previously saved your life are triggered again as automatically as if they had been forged by 10,000 hours of practice.

As a former military pilot, I'm aware of this phenomenon. In pilot training the instructors would put student pilots in simulators and subject us to unsurvivable situations again and again. We would emerge from the simulators dripping in sweat and with our hearts racing. Even though we were just sitting in the simulator working the controls and flipping switches, our bodies responded to the effort like we were doing back-to-back Ironman triathlons. But that's the point. The hormones released by high-stress situations instruct the brain to imprint memories more deeply. Evolution taught us that trick. The caveman who could remember how he escaped a saber-toothed tiger attack had a statistically better shot at surviving the next one.

That's why time slows down in a car crash or while you're getting mugged. The adrenaline coursing through your veins triggers your brain into hyperactive memory storage. Your mind and senses go into overdrive, absorbing every sensory detail with superhuman lucidity and completeness. Because of this, an event that might only last a split second occupies as much mental storage space as an ordinary week or a month. Years later you can recall details, feelings, colors, smells and sounds more vividly than you can remember that morning's breakfast.

Today, I can remember with perfect detail Martin's facial expressions when the rocket exploded overhead. I can specifically recall a spot of whiskers he'd missed shaving that morning. Another time, at a checkpoint on a still-smoldering battlefield in Ukraine in September 2014, a pro-Russian separatist soldier pointed a loaded Kalashnikov in my face as he accused me of working for the CIA. Today, I recall the vein pattern on the soldier's hand. I still see, with unbelievable clarity, his finger wrapped around the trigger, where my life was reduced to a few foot-pounds of pressure.

This hyper-alertness often extends beyond the actual experience that sparked it. For hours, maybe even days after you evade death, life seems… well, how should I put it… *better.*

You laugh easier. Your senses are sharpened. You notice little details in places and things you have seen countless times before. You burst with affection and want to tell friends and family that you love them. You live harder and truer than you ever have before.

And it feels good.

* * *

The evening I returned to Florida from Afghanistan, I drove across the Everglades at sunset. I pulled the car over on the side of the road, stretched out my arms and felt the sun's warmth on my skin. I closed my eyes and could see the glowing red of the fading day's light through my eyelids.

"I feel so alive," I remember thinking. "I wish I could live my whole life like this."

That is post-traumatic stress disorder, or PTSD.

It's the inability of normal life to ever match the amplitude of living that you achieved in war. It's the letdown of survival, and the worry that normal life is just a countdown to a gentle fade-out.

Ask most combat veterans to name the worst experience of their lives, and they'll probably tell you it was war.

But here's the confusing part. When you ask them to choose the best experience of their life, they'll usually say it was war, too.

This is nearly impossible for someone who has never been in war to understand. But the lesson to be gleaned from this confusing truth is essential to understanding the experiences of the 0.4 percent of the US population in the military and the roughly seven percent who are veterans.

Contrary to what most civilians might think, veterans are not broken, and they are not victims. They should not be pitied or looked at with a sad shaking of the head or some reflexive, "Geez, what a shame." Pitying them belittles their experiences and misrepresents the challenges they face after military life.

Combat veterans have experienced a spectrum of emotions whose breadth supersedes the emotional fluctuations of civilian life by a factor you cannot imagine. That's why it's hard to care about normal things when you come back. Ask a vet about this, it's a common feeling. Normal life, whatever that is, seems silly and pointless. It's a gray rerun that leaves you feeling hollow. You live shallow only skipping across the surface of life, never returning to the heights or the depths of what you felt in war.

But PTSD isn't nostalgia. Nostalgia is really just forgetting the bad parts of a memory, and you never forget the bad parts of war. The pain of losing a friend or the images of the dead reflect in everything you see and echo in everything you hear during days of peace.

Yet, even in times of comfort, you find yourself missing the hardships of deployments. The tough times at least made you feel something. And that's what you miss the most—feeling truly alive.

You say things like, "I was happier living in a plywood hooch in Afghanistan with my worldly possessions reduced to whatever fit into a backpack than I am now, living in this apartment, where everything I could ever want is within my grasp."

That's from my brother, Drew, a veteran who now works on Wall Street.

But how does that make sense? Why do the fantasies that sustained us through the toughest times of our lives seem like disappointments when we come home to live them?

Maybe, for those of us who have been to war, the metric by which you measure pleasure and pain is permanently reset. You're not sad. You're just flat. You start to lust for the feelings to which you didn't realize you were addicted, but which required the worst experience of your life to achieve.

You grow resentful of those who go about their lives indifferent to your experiences and the sacrifices of the brothers and sisters with whom you've served. The little pleasures and achievements that drive most people's lives and the challenges they claim to have overcome all seem inconsequential. You see reflections of your wartime experience in every part of life, and you wonder, knowing what you know now, how those around you can live the way they do.

That's PTSD.

Combat veterans aren't damaged. They are enlightened, complicated souls forced to live life by a set of rules and expectations that can make pursuing true happiness feel like chasing the moon.

And for those who ultimately descend into a darkness from which they cannot save themselves, it was not war that broke them.

It was the peace to which they returned, but never found.

1998–2011: War Got in the Way

21 Names

Going to war was never a dream of mine. As a boy I imagined a life of adventures in faraway lands. But war got in the way of those childhood dreams, right at the cusp of making them real. Still, before going to war was ever part of the picture, my ambitions were clear. I wanted to be a pilot.

My parents took me to airshows and sent me to Space Camp. We made childhood pilgrimages to the Smithsonian Air and Space Museum and Kennedy Space Center and my dad took me out to see the US Air Force Academy. As a teenager, I took flying lessons and spent my spare time hanging out with the mechanics and flight instructors at the airport in my hometown of Sarasota, Florida. I soloed on my 16th birthday, the absolute earliest age allowed. My mom's look of terror was unforgettable as she stood on the tarmac and watched me climb all alone into the little, twin-seat Cessna 152—just a few hours, mind you, after I had passed my driving exam. She, through no fault of her own, thought that flying "solo" meant I would be the pilot in command, yet still under the watchful eye of my flight instructor, François (a former French Air Force pilot) in the co-pilot's seat.

Imagine my mother's horror, then, as I waved to her through the cockpit window with a big shit-eating grin on my face, totally alone inside the aircraft with the propeller churning to go. To her credit, she didn't budge, but stayed there on the tarmac alongside my father and François, watching with bated breath as her 16-year-old son took to the skies for a few touch and gos.

After shutting down, I felt like Lindbergh landing in Paris as I climbed out the small plane and into my parents' teary-eyed embraces. As is the tradition, François cut the tail off my T-shirt and signed a congratulatory note on it in marker. Two decades later, that old shirt still hangs in my childhood bedroom.

It would be another two years before I could vote and five more years before I could legally buy a beer. But at 16, I was licensed to both fly a plane and drive a car. I was ahead of the curve.

*   *   *

The first true crossroads in my life was when I read Heinrich Harrer's book, *Seven Years in Tibet*, as a 16-year-old. Soon thereafter, I began to imagine what it would be like to travel through that remote, mountainous land. To be alone in the Himalayas with only a backpack and a camera, silently sitting on some lonely bluff.

Strange daydreams, perhaps, for a 16-year-old from Florida. Yet my Walter Mitty fantasies were about more than the mountains. I was also fascinated by Harrer's personal transformation. His time in the Himalayas among the Tibetan people had transformed him from a brash, ego-driven mountaineer—who was also a Nazi—into a sympathetic witness and lifelong champion for a nation in exile.

The mountains had scraped Harrer clean and rebuilt him into someone else entirely. Even as a 16-year-old, the combined wonder of adventure and promise of self-actualization were irresistible, although to this day I still don't know why those things appealed to me at such an early age. In any case, as my sophomore year of high school ended at the beginning of the summer of 1998, I'd made up my mind. I was going to the Himalayas.

I sat my parents down on the couch and declared to them with triumphant self-confidence that I would go to Nepal and hike to Mount Everest base camp that winter. And, most importantly, I would go alone. That was just two years after the "Into Thin Air" disaster on Everest, and Jon Krakauer's book about it had inspired me to pick Nepal as my destination. Plus, ever since China invaded Tibet in the 1950s foreign tourists could only travel to Tibet while under government escort. That wasn't the sort of adventure I was looking for.

So, Tibet was out. Nepal was in. My parents' approval was the question mark.

Understandably, my parents were reluctant to let me go. To say the least. But with enough cajoling and plenty of promises that I wouldn't do anything too stupid, they eventually conceded. One condition: I would have to raise enough money working jobs over the summer to pay for the airfare. My parents secretly hoped, I now suspect, that a summer spent on a construction site in the Florida heat would put my nomadic ambitions at bay. By that fall, however, I had raised enough dough for a plane ticket to Kathmandu and was all the more determined to see my idea to fruition.

In a monumental act of faith my parents kept their word. Thus, over Christmas break of my junior year of high school, I set off by myself for Kathmandu. Several weeks later, I stood before Mount Everest. With the jingle of a yak train moving behind me, and the cold, high-altitude wind lapping at my neck, I wondered how I could ever describe this place and the people in it to my friends and family back home. I didn't understand so at the time, but I had found my true calling.

It was not, however, a flawless trip, and my parents' reservations about letting loose a wanderlusting 16-year-old unsupervised in Nepal for a month were not altogether unfounded. Although it would be years before I ever told them the whole story.

I had planned to meet a guide in Kathmandu before taking a flight into the mountains together to begin the trek. Well, the thing is, I wasn't scheduled to meet that guide until a few days after my arrival in Kathmandu, leaving me with time to kill in the city on my own beforehand. Before my departure, my parents had wisely made only one rule—I was not to wander alone in Kathmandu before the trek. Predictably, however, my bags had barely hit the hotel room floor before I was out the door and exploring the city. Sorry, Mom and Dad.

I'm not quite sure if my parents truly expected me to sit alone in a hotel room for days on end. But now I understand they were simply searching for a modicum of peace while I was away. Their single rule was a self-soothing act to prove this whole trip wasn't a totally crazy idea, and they needed an alibi for my inevitably bad behavior.

I was, to the credit of my parents' suspicions, woefully naïve and irresponsible. And it was only due to the grace of the best kind of bad luck that I was able to skip through those days without any lifelong repercussions.

One afternoon in those days before the trek, I decided to visit a famous temple in the center of Kathmandu. I hailed a taxi outside the hotel and explained where I wanted to go. The driver enthusiastically and repeatedly replied, "Yes, yes, no problem."

I was on my way, or so I thought.

We weaved through the narrow, chaotic streets, dodging cows, rickshaws, and pedestrians, and were soon climbing through the stair-stepped plots of farmland spread across the mountain bowl in which Kathmandu sits. It slowly dawned on me that we weren't going where I had intended. My confidence muted by youth and inexperience, I hesitated to speak up at first. But I knew something had been seriously lost in translation, and I eventually summoned the courage to question the driver about our destination. I repeated the name of the temple in both English and my bastardized version of Nepali. I even had a pocket map, on which I clearly pointed out where I wished to go.

To all of which the driver nodded his head and robotically repeated his "yes, yes, no problem" mantra.

I understood something wasn't right. No matter how vast the communication gap between us, we both knew full well we were headed the wrong way.

"Why," I then wondered and worried, "was he taking me somewhere else?"

And what waited for me there?

At this point we were well outside the city and beyond the ring road. As we approached a small village, I tried one more time to show the driver on the map where I wanted to go.

I received another round of head nods and "yes, yes, no problem" dismissals. To my everlasting credit, I simply thought, "fuck it," as I kicked open the door to the moving taxi and jumped out. Only a few bruises and dusty clothes the worse, I leapt over the guardrail and stumbled down the mountainside at the fastest clip I could manage. I never looked back, convinced that I'd just narrowly escaped a kidnapping plot and was surely being chased. Of course, it's entirely possible there was nothing nefarious about that cab ride. But, I must say, sometimes it's better to leave a question mark in your past rather than know for sure that your worst suspicions were true.

For the rest of that afternoon and into the evening I descended through the terraced farmland, passing, from time to time, through the small, austere villages that dotted the way back to Kathmandu's city limits. It was clear that few tourists drifted through this area, based on the greeting I received in each little hamlet. People rushed out into the dirt streets, politely and cheerfully pestering me with textbook English phrases like, "Hello, sir, nice to meet you… Where are you from? How are you getting on?"

At 16, I was already 6 feet 2 inches tall, thin and pale-skinned with a long shock of blond hair. I was, I suspect, the perfect stereotype of what those Nepali villagers imagined a foreigner to be.

One memory from that day, which has stayed with me more than any other, was the sight of two children, a boy and a girl, playing amid a pile of trash. I can still see their bare feet in the decaying rubbish, the blotches of dirt on their exposed legs, their tattered clothes, and matted, unwashed hair.

I've come across much more disturbing, brutal scenes in my life since then, but that was the moment in which I first, truly realized how fortunate I was. I never saw the world the same way again.

By dusk I had made it back to the ring road highway around Kathmandu. Staring through the headlights that scattered into obscurity through Kathmandu's ever-present haze of dust and pollution, I was able to hail a taxi and, for the first time that day, successfully communicate where I wanted to go.

"Back to the Shangri-La Hotel," I declared. And back to the Shangri-La Hotel we went.

That night, I wrote in my journal:

"The culture here is so radically different than anything I have ever seen. The contrast between this world and the one I am used to at home almost makes this place seem unreal, it seems as if a place like this could not really exist."

Again, I was growing up fast.

*   *   *

On Christmas Eve of 1998, I arrived, winded from the thin air, in the de facto Sherpa capital of Namche Bazaar. At an altitude of 11,286 feet, the village sits atop a bluff at the head of the Imja Khola river valley. From a ridge above Namche Bazaar, you can see up the long valley to the black peak of Everest, which juts into the jet stream three and a half miles above you. A nearly permanent banner of wind blasts snow trails from the highest summit on Earth in static motion like a comet's tail.

That Christmas Eve was the first I had ever spent apart from my family, and I managed to score a few minutes on a New Zealand mountaineering group's satellite phone (a rarity in 1998). My parents were elated, of course, to hear my staticky voice from a faraway Himalayan village—this was still the era before iPhones and Facebook, and I was more or less off the grid while abroad.

For my part, I brimmed with excitement and pride, feeling like some sort of conquering hero to call back home from so far away. Truly, however, I was simply lonely and grasping for a connection to home as I economically explained to my parents what Mount Everest looked like at sunset.

"We had our Christmas Eve celebration tonight," I wrote in my journal. "It was very festive with gift exchanges between us and the

Sherpas, as well as caroling and a cake prepared by Pemba. I was a little sad to be away from my family, though. It was not only an emotional time because of the holidays, but because of what I'm doing and where I am. And I really want to talk with someone about it."

The next time I would spend Christmas Eve apart from my parents would be 11 years after I wrote those words. Again, I would be in the mountains. In fact, a geologic extension of the same ones I had trekked through as a 16-year-old. That second Christmas Eve away from my family, all those years later, would be just as epically significant as the first. But for vastly different reasons.

*   *   *

With memories of the Himalayas fresh in my mind I returned home to Florida and resumed my junior year of high school. Reuniting with friends, I sensed I had aged a decade in the few weeks I was away. Thus, when it came time to choose a university, I wanted something extraordinary. My top priority was a career path that promised a lifetime of adventure. Flying was still the game plan, and the US Air Force Academy fit the bill. So, three weeks after graduating from high school, I boarded a plane to Colorado Springs with two months of basic training and a decade in the military before me.

Because that seed of adventure was planted in me so early, every so often I've felt the need to rediscover, or relive, what I had felt as a 16-year-old in the Himalayas. I was lucky to have discovered something about which I was so passionate. But it was a curse, too, because that passion ultimately swelled to supersede all the other things that mattered, like family, friends, and finances. It was to become a lifetime imbalance, perennially estranging me from the people who loved me. All to re-experience the first hit of the drug of adventure that I'd felt as a 16-year-old. The problem with any drug, however, is that you have to continually up the dosage to feel the same high. And the tragedy of the euphoria you get from traveling is that it doesn't last. It might stay with you for a year, or maybe a bit longer, but it's easy to forget when the realities of day-to-day life inevitably clutter your mind.

Or when a war gets in the way.

* * *

When I entered the Air Force Academy in June of 2000, I was 18 years old. My application essay spoke of adventure, travel, exotic experiences, and a career distant from the confines of a desk. At that time, war was an abstraction. An impossibility. And I wasn't alone in thinking so.

In 2000 the country was still absorbed in post–Cold War delusions about everlasting peace. During my freshman year at the Academy we discussed Francis Fukuyama's famous essay, "The End of History," and earnestly debated whether the US would ever go to war again. The Soviet Union had collapsed and the Cold War was over. We'd won. Now, it was a unipolar world with America on top of the geopolitical totem pole.

Everything changed on September 11, 2001, of course.

"A plane flew into the World Trade Center," I overheard someone say on the walk to class that morning.

"What an idiot," was his friend's response, assuming with the typical bravado of an Air Force Academy cadet that it was an accident on the part of some careless civilian pilot.

I didn't give the comment much thought, I remember. It was a clear autumn morning in Colorado, just as it was in New York City. I crossed the massive outdoor courtyard of the Air Force Academy, known as the terrazzo, passing by fighter jets on permanent display and a polished black stone memorial to graduates killed in combat. In 2001 the memorial hadn't been added to in a while. Most of the engraved names were from Vietnam and had been faded and worn dull by time.

The faces of the cadets that morning offered no clue to the drama unfolding across the country. We stared blankly ahead as we trudged to class, our minds filled with worries about homework, military inspections, and fitness tests. I entered Fairchild Hall, the Air Force

Academy's academic building, and a few twists, turns, and staircases later I was at the door to my 7:30 a.m. political science class. I passed the threshold from the hallway to the classroom. No more than three feet, just one step. But that step changed everything. By the time I lifted my foot and placed it on the floor inside the classroom, I'd left behind the naïve dreams of youth and had met for the first time the reality of a new world and the conflict that would consume the next decade of my life. I took that step and the burning towers were on TV and I knew it meant war.

*   *   *

The previous day, I had visited a chaplain. I told him I wanted to quit the academy. I hated it, I confessed. I didn't understand why I was there getting yelled at every day for not shining my shoes correctly while my friends were back at the University of Florida wearing flip-flops and crashing sorority parties. Why did I have to take 21 credit hours a semester and learn how to march when I could go to regular college and have a class or two a day and spend my free time lounging poolside? I was feeling extremely sorry for myself. The chaplain suggested the military wasn't for me. Maybe I was there for the wrong reasons.

That night I went to my room and filled out an application to transfer to the University of Florida for the spring 2002 semester. That application was on my desk, completely filled out, when I walked to class the morning of September 11, 2001.

"The world is going to change," the political science instructor said to us as we watched the towers fall.

"Every one of you will go to war," he said with sureness, adding, "And some of you won't come back."

Heavy stuff for a 19-year-old. But he was right.

When I got back to my room that afternoon, I sent a message to my family that I was okay. And then I took that transfer application to the University of Florida in my hand. It felt toxic to touch. I was

Here I am in Air Force pilot training in 2009 alongside my whip—the supersonic T-38C Talon jet trainer.

embarrassed by it—an artifact of a time to which I could never return. The carefree life of travel and adventure I had dreamt of and longed for was now a shattered illusion. I crumpled the letter and was about to throw it away, but hesitated and then spread the paper back flat on my desk. I used a Sharpie marker to write the word "remember" across the top before I locked it away.

Years later, I brought that old, wrinkled paper with me when I went back to the Air Force Academy as a 36-year-old civilian. I had it in my pocket when, with my wife, Lilly, at my side, I visited the polished black stone monument to the fallen and dragged my fingers across the 21 freshly carved names.

Holidays

The first time I ever saw war was on Christmas Eve in 2009. At the time, I was a green Air Force special operations pilot on my first deployment to Afghanistan.

I had already been in-country for a few weeks, flying mostly day missions. Easy stuff, like surveillance and reconnaissance sorties, which typically meant orbiting ad infinitum over a target while on autopilot.

I'd usually bring an energy drink in the boot pocket of my tan flight suit as a pick-me-up before landing. During the missions, which lasted for hours, I'd munch on sandwiches I'd picked up from the chow hall before takeoff.

Truly, up to that point, the flying I had done over Afghanistan wasn't much different than training missions back at Hurlburt Field, Florida, where I was then stationed. Except for the mountains, of course, and the ever-present knowledge that the enemy was somewhere down in that maze of patchwork brown and tan fields and stair-stepped plots of vertiginous earth.

Also, the body armor vest and loaded pistol on my chest and the M-4 carbine stashed behind my seat reminded me in no uncertain terms that this was something more serious than a training mission. Still, I hadn't seen the war yet. Not really. I had to tell myself that it was down there.

Properly broken in with the easy missions, for that Christmas Eve sortie I was paired with an older, more experienced pilot as my aircraft commander. For the sake of discretion, I'm not going to mention his name since he's still on active duty. But I will say that he had been an A-10 "Warthog" attack pilot before joining Air Force Special Operations Command, and he knew a lot about war.

As we stepped to the aircraft at Bagram Air Base at dusk, with the distant Hindu Kush mountains painted purple in the dim light of the setting sun, the aircraft commander looked back to me and smiled.

"Awesome, isn't it?" he said.

It was, I said.

That night, we would provide overwatch for a special operations team that was going to helicopter in and assault a compound where a Taliban leader was supposedly holed up. Capture or kill. That was the mission. I muttered Alan Shepard's prayer under my breath as we took off.

Dear Lord, please don't let me fuck up.

Soon, it was night and we were watching the target compound through our high-tech sensors. The darkness of the cockpit amplified the rhythmic drone of the engine and the white noise of the slipstream. Outside, the night sky was simply black to my naked eyes. Yet, when I lowered my night-vision goggles, it was like shining a green-glowing spotlight on the world. Under night vision, I could see the massive mountains beneath us; the snow on their slopes radiated like green lava through the lenses. Above everything, meteors streaked across the sky in a never-ending shimmer like moonlight on the sea.

All of the sudden, we heard the dreaded acronym, "TIC," on the radio.

Troops in contact.

An American ground unit was taking fire miles away from where we were. The voice of the JTAC (the soldier who directs combat aircraft actions from the battlefield) down in the firefight came through the radio with a lot of background noise.

He spoke in short bursts in between his measured, heavy breathing. Nevertheless, I remember feeling impressed by how calm his voice sounded and how precisely he pronounced his words when requesting the airstrike.

The ridgeline where the battle was taking place was off to our right, and we were on the portion of our orbit closest to that spot when we heard the pilot of an American fighter jet radio that he'd released a bomb.

My aircraft commander told me in which direction to look out the side window. At his suggestion, I flipped up my night-vision goggles to stare into the black night with my naked eyes, straining to make out the murky silhouettes of the mountains below.

Then, a flash and a glowing orange orb rose from the earth like a miniature sunrise.

I won't pretend to remember exactly what was said on the radio at that instant, but it was something to the effect of: "The enemies are dead, the Americans are okay."

I do remember one remark, however. I'll never forget it.

"Merry Christmas," someone said.

Later on that night, after a handful of Taliban militants escaped our target compound—"squirters," as we called them—I helped the special operations team track them down. No Americans were wounded or killed.

*   *   *

After returning to base, I relaxed in my bunk and wrote in my journal. I reflected on that night, reeling with its significance. After all the years of training I was there in Afghanistan as a US military pilot flying combat missions.

That night was the first time I had ever seen a weapon fired in anger. It was also the first time I had ever watched people die. Admittedly, it had been a tepid first sip of the combat experience. My life had never been in danger, and I had only seen war from afar, listening on the radio as some of the most lethal warriors in human history—American fighter pilots and special operations troops—killed their enemies. Still, I had contributed, albeit microscopically, to the war effort. I had been useful.

Every Christmas Eve thereafter, I've thought about that night in Afghanistan. Especially as my wartime experiences, both as a pilot and a war correspondent, have accumulated over the years, becoming a recurrent theme in my life.

Holidays, after all, are perennial markers of time's passage through which we can take stock of how little or how much life has changed each intervening year. For that reason, when Christmas comes around it doesn't escape me that American troops are still deployed around the world, some in myriad combat zones while others conduct training missions in allied nations, providing a valuable deterrent against military aggression.

For American military personnel, such deployments are no longer an interruption of normal life, but a predictable part of it. A recurrent marker of the passage of time as perpetual as the holidays. Active-duty US troops of my generation have spent their adult lives rotating between combat zone deployments. Yet, for their part, many of the younger troops can't even remember the world before September 11, 2001.

The last time the United States celebrated a true peacetime Christmas was the year 2000. I was then halfway through my freshman year at the US Air Force Academy, on leave for the holidays in Sarasota.

I remember how proud I was when I stepped off the airplane in my uniform and saw my family waiting for me at the end of the jet bridge, as you could still do those days. I was just 18 years old and slowly adjusting to military life. Yet going to war was never part of the picture. I seriously wondered whether my country would ever go to war again. Nine months later I knew for certain we would. And every year after that, we've had troops deployed in war zones for the holidays.

These days, I have all the respect in the world for the young American men and women who volunteer for military service. They know exactly what they're getting into. I also wonder if America will ever celebrate another peacetime Christmas in my lifetime. It's not called the "forever war" for nothing. But at some point, every individual soldier stops going to war, even if it's still there. At some point, each

US soldier, sailor, airman, or Marine will privately wonder—*Have I done enough?*

When is it right to go on living, even while the wars go on and on?

* * *

People often ask me about the difficulties of writing about war. They want to know if it's hard to remain upbeat after seeing so many terrible things. Truthfully, the answer is yes, sometimes it's tough. It's hard to care about the normal, trivial problems of life after witnessing how much people suffer in war.

Sometimes, when the holidays roll around, and the wars go on and on, I wonder what's worth celebrating. But I also remember something else I've learned over the years from my wartime experiences. War brings out the most beautiful parts of humanity, too. In war, you see instances of total selflessness, of men and women willing to sacrifice everything for invisible ideas like freedom and justice, or to protect their families and their comrades. Sometimes, to protect people they've never even met.

Perhaps, in the end, war is as perennial as any holiday and always will be. But so are other things like hope, love, and the unending willingness of good people to stand up against evil.

Each Christmas, that's something to celebrate.

Culture Shock

In the summer of 2011, when I announced my decision to leave the military, my family and friends thought I was crazy.

"Just stick it out another 10 years and make it to retirement," was a common piece of advice.

"You're a fool to leave a steady paycheck and free health care," others warned. "The job market is awful right now."

I was resistant to the idea that I should stay in the military for job security, and my mind was set on getting out. By 2011, I had spent most of my youth either training to go to war or in it. I'd been a top Air Force Academy graduate, a graduate student at the Sorbonne in Paris, and an Air Force captain and special operations pilot with combat deployments around the world. I'd finished an Ironman triathlon and had run a marathon across a glacier in Antarctica. Yet it wasn't enough. You see, I wanted to live the life of adventure that I'd dreamt of before war got in the way. I wanted to explore the world unbound from the rules and confines of military life. But there was more to it than that. I was also anxious to finally exercise the artistic, romantic parts of my personality, which I had suppressed for the sake of my military career.

In short, there were other things I wanted to do with my life and I was ready to move on. But the warnings I received about the transition to civilian life were not unfounded. The job market was a tough one in 2011, only three years after the 2008 financial crash. Plus, starting life over again from scratch at 29 years old wasn't easy, even without the Great Recession to deal with. For one, the entire identity I had created in my twenties—that of an Air Force pilot—essentially vanished overnight. I was, in some ways, back to where I had been at 18. With a clean slate, yes, and that felt rejuvenating. But there was also an unshakeable expectation that I should be much further along in life.

With my uniforms now folded and packed away and my hair getting longer, I found myself wondering, "Now what?"

I waffled. First, I thought about joining the Peace Corps. I even went as far as receiving an assignment to Moldova, but backed out at the last minute, thinking I shouldn't waste time on an experience that wasn't a stepping stone to a new career. My parents pushed for law school, and some friends said I should get a job as a military contractor or a commercial pilot.

I rejected all those ideas.

At heart, I was still that 16-year-old, fresh from the Himalayas with wild dreams about travel and adventure. But going to war had complicated my adolescent lust for adventure. Experience for its own sake was no longer enough—I needed a purpose, too.

I'd learned by then that many dark forces in the world are held at bay by a thinner margin than those of us who have only known peace in our lives can possibly understand. I remember coming home from Iraq and Afghanistan and observing the glazed-over look in people's eyes when I tried to explain for them what I had seen and done in those distant war zones. And yet, I repeatedly tried to make the unimaginable seem real through words alone. The truth is, I'd gone to war and come home with a story to tell. Thus, I made up my mind that a career in journalism promised the kind of meaningful, exciting life for which I was looking. I'd found my new path.

That summer, I applied to Northwestern University's Medill School of Journalism. And then, on the cusp of a whole new life with endless new possibilities, I decided to return to the roof of the world.

*   *   *

I sold my car, threw everything I owned in a storage unit and bought a one-way ticket from Tampa, Florida to New Delhi, India. Beyond that, I had only a direction, not a destination, in mind. Maybe some of that lost currency of youth was recoverable, after all.

And, although I had not yet come to terms with it at the time, I was also in search of forgiveness. As a pilot, I'd never experienced killing in the way a soldier on the ground does. For me, killing was a flip of a switch, the pushing of a button, or a word spoken on the radio. It was never personal. And I rarely questioned the utility of the way in which I contributed to the war. Yet, sometimes, innocents died, and I was hard pressed to examine my actions when that happened. Some things are hard to forget, or forgive.

It was so easy for others to tell me that such things happen in war, and I should move on. But that advice came from people who'd never been to war. Their advice was thoughtfully considered and sincere, but it was also useless.

It's easy to spot those brave people who bear the physical wounds of war. What's harder to see, and much harder for those who have only known peace in their lives to understand, is that sometimes people come back from war with amputated souls. And there's no prosthetic for that.

*   *   *

On the evening of my first full day in India, I ordered a bottle of wine to quench my thirst and dilute my mixed emotions. A few glasses into my second bottle, and I was reeling from the combined effects of alcohol and culture shock.

Adjusting to a new culture had never been such a struggle. There was simply nothing familiar about that place. The culture, religion, and innumerable little differences in the way of life all combined into a cultural shockwave that left me stunned and stupid. I had taken it for granted that I'd be able to effortlessly flow into the rootless life of a nomad. The trip, needless to say, was not the carefree adventure for which I had hoped. Exotic places, for all their romantic appeal, are usually somewhat of a letdown when you cross the threshold from fantasy to reality. In that way, coming home from war was a lot like walking alone in a foreign country.

I was still very much in that "pendulum swing" moment after the military. I wasn't shaving, my hair hadn't seen a barber in months. I was like a snake shedding his skin. But without the military, I worried, who was I?

A few weeks earlier, I had been in Chicago to interview for the graduate program at Medill. I'd spent a few nights there alone, wandering the streets with no destination in mind. I noticed minute details because my thoughts were drawn inward and I was hypersensitive to this foreign world around me. Through the windows of restaurants and bars I observed groups of friends, couples on dates, young people effortlessly enjoying their lives in a way that seemed so impossible for me to do. I felt jealous, bitter even. I wasn't envious for what everyone else had, only that they could so easily enjoy it. I was always the traveler, even in places that should feel like home.

Winter 2011:
Mountains and Dreams

The Enemy

My younger brother, Drew, told me one of the worst stories I've yet to hear from the wars in Iraq and Afghanistan.

An Air Force officer at the time, he was riding in a convoy from Bagram Air Base to Kabul during a deployment to Afghanistan in August 2010.

This particularly dangerous stretch of road was known as "suicide alley" due to the frequency of Taliban improvised explosive device attacks. Most of the IEDs the Taliban used were physically connected to detonators by a thin copper "piano wire," which made them immune to jamming and particularly lethal.

These hard-wired IEDs required precision from the attacker to time the explosion with passing vehicles. So the best defense was to drive fast and not stop—no matter what.

"The Taliban would do anything to get us to stop," Drew later told me. "But as soon as you stop or open your door, you're dead."

My brother was in the lead vehicle of the convoy that day. Drew was sitting in the back left seat of the Toyota Tacoma behind the Afghan National Police officer who was driving. There were two other people in the truck's cab, as well as another Afghan National Police officer with a Kalashnikov in the back bed.

Suddenly, there was the high-pitched squeal of brakes and the deep bass thump of impact. Drew instinctively faced forward, only to see a girl split in two over the hood of the truck.

"Half her body went over the truck, half her body went under it," as he described it.

There was a lot of blood. People inside the truck were yelling and cussing. The guy in the front passenger seat yelled, "Go, go, go."

"We just ran over a fucking kid," someone else said.

The Afghan driver fought through his instinct to stop the truck. He knew this was no accident.

The driver later explained that he saw a man kick the girl into the road. This was a tactic the Taliban used to set up ambushes on NATO and Afghan government convoys. But the driver didn't fall for the ploy. He punched the gas and kept the truck moving, thus saving the lives of my brother and everyone else inside from the ambush that was sure to follow.

"It messed with our heads," Drew said. "But I'm sure if we stopped, they had some plans for us."

Six years later, Drew's sentences sometimes faded into a whisper as he explained that day, his mind replaying images and sounds no words can recreate. That kind of barbarity wounds the souls and consciences of the troops who witness it.

"It definitely makes you question whether we are doing more harm than good over there," Drew said. "Who are these people, the Taliban? These are not human beings. There is no bringing these people back. And if they are willing to do this to win, there is no bomb that can defeat that."

He inhaled like a doctor about to deliver a terminal diagnosis. At length he let out his breath and said, "How do you destroy someone who doesn't care about being destroyed?"

We've all seen the images of American World War II veterans together with their former German and Japanese enemies, sharing a moment of mutual respect for the common experience of spending one's youth in war. I must confess, it once felt impossible to believe that I could ever find such common ground, or humanity, with a veteran of the Taliban. Especially after the stories of savagery I've heard from other veterans like my brother. How could I ever find common ground with someone who represented pure evil?

It's impossible.

That's what I thought, anyway.

* * *

With the first of the sun, we descended out of the arid, lifeless landscape of India's Himalayan Ladakh region and entered the verdant mountain world of Kashmir. On the way into Srinagar, the summer capital of India's Jammu and Kashmir state, we passed grassy fields and river rapids with forested mountains overhead. I was reminded of the Alps in summertime Switzerland or Austria. But as we drove through villages perched peacefully within the forested valleys, we also passed patrols of Indian Army units with guns drawn, with one poor sap up front waving a metal detector. Evidence of something evil beneath the surface.

Srinagar sat on the marshy, subtropical shores of Dal Lake. Forested, snow-capped mountains lined the horizon and the air was sticky hot and hazy. I walked from my hotel along a road called the Broadway, which followed the lakeshore into an inlet with an idyllic view across the lake. Ornate wooden houseboats lined the quays, and the emerald green surface of the water was sprinkled with small rowboats called *shikaras*, somewhat equivalent in size and shape to Venice's gondolas. Most men were bearded and wore head covers and the traditional shalwar kameez outfit. Women were typically under a burka or veiled.

Despite its natural beauty, the area was clearly on edge. Kashmir has been a battleground between India and Pakistan since 1947, when the two countries split following independence from the United Kingdom. The inclusion of Islamic Kashmir within Hindu India angered the powers-that-be in Pakistan who felt the land was rightfully theirs. Guerrilla wars and constant violence have plagued the region ever since.

The Indian army's presence was ubiquitous in Srinagar. Armed soldiers patrolled the streets with Kalashnikovs slung over their shoulders. Armored personnel carriers were positioned at intersections across town. The day prior to my arrival, a bomb detonated at a financial office in Delhi, killing 15. A Kashmiri group claimed responsibility, and the Indian military consequently cracked down in Srinagar.

As squads of Indian soldiers patrolled the streets, people stood in doorways with arms crossed, watching. There was no active unrest, but the insoluble coexistence of the Indian military and the local population reminded me of two armies camped in trenches on opposite sides of no man's land. For a US military veteran looking to distance himself from the wars in Iraq and Afghanistan, this was a poor choice for a vacation. A feeling of uneasiness loomed over me like Pig-Pen's cloud. I was, naturally and automatically, on edge. Yet, I rejected those impulses as best I could, having traveled enough to know that people should not be judged by the actions of a few, or their past. People from any two cultures are likely to find some common, human attribute that can oppose the gravitational pull of our uncivilized instincts. But something about Kashmir tempted me to overlook the journeyer's relativistic mindset. It was the glaring eyes, I think.

On the evening of my arrival in Srinagar, I walked down to the lakeshore and hired an oarsman for a sunset *shikara* ride. It was peaceful on the water amid the late-day stillness and the airbrushed light of sunset. We traveled through a series of canals, where entire villages were built on wood pilings along the marshy shores. We pulled off at one dock and bought apples from an old man. Nearby, a group of children took turns jumping into the water. As we made our way back out into the heart of the lake, the young oarsman explained to me how happy he was that I had decided to visit Kashmir. He implored me to tell my friends about its beauty. Yet, as he spoke, I noticed for the first time the words "death to the Zionist pigs" crudely scratched into the wooden floor of the boat. And there it was again, that subtle undertone of hate. As omnipresent as the humidity, it permeated everything, spoiling even the sincerest smile.

After the ride, the *shikara* oarsman deposited me back along the Broadway quay. I thanked him and tipped him generously. He made me promise I'd stop by to see him again before I left. I never did.

*   *   *

One day in Srinagar, with little to do, I decided to buy a necklace as a souvenir for my girlfriend at the time. I went into town in search of a jewelry store and found a place along the lakeshore. I went inside and browsed the shelves, looking for something beautiful. Kashmir is famous for its gemstones, and the jewelry on display was of vivid colors, swirled and dotted like the colored sky in "The Starry Night."

I chose a bracelet and went to pay. The young man working the counter seemed about my age. Slim, with dark hair and complexion, and a short, scruffy beard, he had on blue jeans and a white button-down shirt and smiled broadly as I approached.

I asked the bracelet's price, and he responded in flawless, British-accented English. After I paid, the young man asked what I was doing in Kashmir. I replied in total earnestness, explaining how I had just left a career in the military and was on a journey to chart the course of the rest of my life. The man, quietly and with a serious, focused expression, listened to me. And then, when I had finished talking, he poured us both a cup of tea and put out a plate of cookies.

"I was a soldier too," he said.

He looked at me with a calm, confident demeanor and waited for my inevitable follow-on question.

"Yes?" I replied. "Was it for the Indian army?"

He told me he had fought for the Taliban in Afghanistan.

There was a heavy silence.

Our postures hardened, more from amazement at this unlikely situation than actual animosity. We two enemies—uncertain, then, whether former or current—considered each other.

"Who is the bracelet for?" he asked at last.

"My girlfriend."

"Is she in America?"

"Yes." I asked him, "Are you married?"

"Yes, and we have a daughter."

Something was coming down between us; a question had been answered.

Had we seen each other in the war, we would have surely tried to kill each other. We had been enemies, and neither of us would have given it a second thought. Yet, here we were. Two young men. Talking to each other as any two young men would.

I asked about his daughter and what she was like. He told me how she liked to read and sing. He said he walked her to the school bus each morning; it was a guaranteed way to spend time with her. He was afraid of not having enough time with her, he added.

He wanted to know about Florida, where I had grown up. We didn't talk about the war, but the war wasn't an obstacle between us. It was, in fact, a unifying thing. A shared experience, with all the inherent psychological baggage that only someone who has been in war could know. We instantly and effortlessly understood each other.

He told me that after leaving Afghanistan he had made his way into Indian Kashmir to join his extended family. He left the war in search of a life in peace. I knew what it took to leave the war behind, so I already knew a lot about him.

The war was our bond, even if we had once been enemies. And truly, we still were. I had friends fighting in Afghanistan, and the man likely had comrades still among the Taliban, although I didn't ask. He spoke disdainfully of Islamic extremism and seemed to have renounced the Taliban's cause, although we didn't talk about that, either.

Enthusiastically, the young man told me about Kashmir. He mused over the various mountain hikes, how beautiful the high alpine meadows were in the summer and how good the skiing was in the winter. He seemed to have found a peaceful existence, anchored in love for his family and the beauty of the mountains.

A shikara boat on Srinigar's Dal Lake in Indian Kashmir. Despite the area's beauty, there was a subtle undertone of violence due to an ongoing Islamist insurgency.

War, as I would later discover as a conflict journalist, is never black and white. As a soldier, you try to see it that way, even if you know it's not true. Thoughtfully considering your enemy's humanity or the circumstances in life that led him or her to the opposing side of the battlefield are dangerous habits to get into. It contradicts your belief in absolutes like good and evil, the justice of your cause, and your immunity from the moral consequences of killing in combat. To consider your enemy as a human being is to judge each act of violence in war as a singular event for which you must atone.

Killing in war is not typically personal; it's a blind thrust done into the ether of the conflict, propelled by reasons that have nothing to do with the character of the person you're trying to kill. The lives lost on the other side are attributable to the war, not you.

You don't think about the life stories of your enemies. On the screen inside the cockpit, white blobs glow against a black background. Exploding, disintegrating, folding to the ground, disappearing in flashes. Dying. But those aren't men like this one standing in front of you in the jewelry shop; they are only the necessary braids woven into the tapestry of winning the war.

Now I was in the gray zone that either haunts or releases you after war. Here I was, face to face with my enemy. A man I would have killed without hesitation. And the same went for him toward me. Yet, we were both veterans now, able to share a cup of tea. We talked like two men who were in the first tentative exchanges of becoming friends. I asked him about fatherhood, and he asked about my family in America.

Perhaps, as soldiers, the farther we get from the bullets and the bombs the more we realize that the true enemy is the war itself. War is a monster, collectively released, and it is the monster we fight against, not each other.

It felt good, in a way, to be friendly to that young man in the jewelry shop. As if this expression of humanity was proof that, although my soul had been bent, it was not too far gone to regain its original shape. We acted like the war had never happened. But I wonder now whether we could have been so friendly, so easily, if we had never been enemies.

The young man made me promise to return to Kashmir one day. He even offered to let me stay at his home. I thanked him and sincerely promised him I would.

I felt elated at our parting. But it didn't last.

At the time of writing, American troops are still fighting and dying in Afghanistan and that man is still my enemy. Our wars aren't over yet, even if we don't go to them anymore.

I haven't returned to Kashmir. Although I hope to one day, now that I know what's waiting for me there.

Scars

After Kashmir, I wandered for months, crisscrossing India and Nepal. The journey was everything I had hoped it would be. I studied Buddhism in the misty mountain village of McLeod Ganj in India, the seat of the Tibetan government in exile. Later, while in Nepal, I hiked alone for weeks in the Annapurna region.

As winter neared, I returned to Kathmandu and plotted the final chapter of my adventures. I had come up with a plan and it was this: I would return to the Khumbu region and retrace the route I had taken as a 16-year-old. After several weeks of solo trekking, I intended to reach the village of Chukhung where a Sherpa guide would lead me on a climb up Island Peak, a 20,305-foot-high side spur of Mount Everest.

Climbing Island Peak would be a serious adventure. The mountain is as high as Denali; its slopes are steep and icy, requiring the use of crampons and ice axes. It would be unlike any other physical challenge I had yet experienced. The purpose, of course, wasn't to *conquer* anything. Many people had already done what I was about to do. Ultimately, the point was to suffer, and hopefully learn something in the process.

* * *

The trek began with an early morning flight to the village of Lukla. Just as I remembered it, landing in this mountain village was both a thrilling and a horrifying experience. In fact, as a former military pilot, I was now more aware of the actual dangers than I had been at 16. My knuckles, consequently, were a little whiter this time around as we lurched to a stop on the short, steep runway.

I hiked for weeks, living out of a backpack like a true nomad. I loved the simplicity and raw physicality of this lifestyle. It was a way of living so far removed from the normal routine of modern life that it awoke within me a sense of strength and health that had long been dormant. The freedom from worry was equally as energizing. I had brought no gadgets with me, so I was cut off from the internet, email, and phone calls. I was totally rooted in the present, so no energy was wasted on what might happen beyond tomorrow. There was no schedule to keep, no calendar to reference for daily obligations. I woke with the sun and went to bed at dark. My body was in tune with the outside world, my mind entrenched in the here and now.

*　　*　　*

The final night before the Island Peak climb, I was in the dining room of the lodge in Chukhung, Nepal, eating Tibetan *momos* while I sipped on an Everest beer. I had just begun a conversation with a Canadian climber about my time in Afghanistan as an Air Force pilot when I heard an American voice call out from across the dark, smoky room: "Dude, were you in the US military?"

Through the haze of burning yak dung fueling the stove around which we sat, I saw a young, bearded man. He wore a black beanie and his short sleeves revealed arms covered in tattoos. There were scars beneath the ink. I'd seen arms like those before on my brothers in Afghanistan and Iraq. Before he said another word, I knew he was an American soldier, and I knew he was special ops.

I politely excused myself from the conversation with the Canadian and joined the man at his table. We made introductions and hit it off immediately. The man's name was Kevin, and he was there with his father who sat beside him.

Like me, they were on their way to climb Island Peak, a 20,305-foot-high side spur of Mount Everest. Kevin and his father were with a guided group run by Adventure Consultants, the company of the ill-fated mountaineering guide, Rob Hall, who had famously telephoned his wife as he lay dying on the summit ridge of Everest to choose a name for their unborn daughter.

I told Kevin and his father that I had been in the US military and served in Iraq and Afghanistan. I had just separated from the Air Force three months earlier, I explained, and was on a trip through India and Nepal, looking for closure.

A light flicked on in Kevin's eyes as I spoke. Conversation burst out of him like he had been slowly filling up for years with the words, waiting to tell his story to someone who might understand.

Kevin had served multiple tours in Iraq and Afghanistan as an Army Ranger, he told me, and he had seen the worst kind of fighting in both places. He described how a terrorist's bomb had decapitated his best friend just yards outside the gates of a base in Afghanistan.

"I had been talking to him just five minutes before that," Kevin said as he scooped a handful of salty popcorn from a bowl on the table between us. "His body was completely fucked up. You couldn't even tell it was him."

Kevin was at a tough time in his life. The war had taken everything from him. His life had fallen apart, bit by bit, and he was in search of a way to put it all back together. Not long after his best friend died, Kevin was himself badly wounded by an improvised explosive device. Shortly thereafter, while recovering from his wounds at a hospital in Germany, he learned that his mother had committed suicide. A few months later, after he had returned to the US, his wife divorced him and took their daughter.

The Army had recently medically discharged Kevin against his will because of his injuries. So, there he was in Nepal, looking to start over and reconnect with his father. What else was there to do? Where else was there to go?

In the book *Eiger Dreams*, Jon Krakauer wrote, "Mountains make poor receptacles for dreams." I suppose he was right, since I never found any answers in the mountains to the questions in my life. But sometimes there just wasn't anywhere else to go when everything fell apart. The mountains may not solve any problems, but the ones they create are simple and free from the complicated tragedies of the lives we leave behind. For Kevin, the mountains were the only place where the world still made sense.

Kevin's dad said good night and wisely went to get some much-needed rest before the big day. We were going to climb a Himalayan mountain the next night. But Kevin and I stayed up, choosing not to worry about the climb. Instead, we kept drinking beer and sharing stories. At one point he asked me what call sign I used in combat.

"Draco," I told him.

Kevin's shoulders slumped forward, his chest deflated and his lips trembled as he spoke: "Are you fucking kidding me?"

And then he started to cry. And trust me, tears looked pretty out of place on Kevin's face. I sat there, stunned and immeasurably curious as to what this was all about, until Kevin began to explain. He was in a firefight in Afghanistan in 2010—a bad one—when he radioed for help. A plane responded and directed the air strike that killed the Taliban fighters about to overrun his position.

"That plane saved my life, and the lives of my men," Kevin told me, his eyes welling.

And then came the kicker. Kevin told me the pilot's call sign.

"Draco," he said. "I've never forgotten."

I was deployed to Afghanistan at the same time his story took place, but it was probably other pilots from my squadron on the mission, I reasoned, since we all used the same call sign in combat. But it could have been me. For Kevin, it didn't matter if it was me or not. I represented that anonymous, airborne vessel of his salvation. The impossible answer to his prayer. He never knew the identity of the pilots who saved him, or even the type of plane they flew since it was all still classified at that time. All he knew was the voice of "Draco" on the radio when he thought he was going to die.

He bought me another beer as a way of saying thanks. Something he had wanted to do for a long time, he told me. He had no reason to thank me, I answered. The truth was, my war had been nothing like Kevin's. I mostly spent it in the relative security of a cockpit, with the ugliness of combat reduced to amorphous infrared images on my displays. But after deploying and serving my country, I think I was there in Nepal for the same reasons as Kevin. I wanted to divorce myself completely and cleanly from the life I had been living, with the hope that this experience could compensate for what I thought I had lost and inspire me to live in a way that was worthy of the second chance not all of my friends would get.

So here we were. Two men who unknowingly depended on each other in combat, meeting for the first time on the eve of climbing a remote Himalayan peak. Together at the end of the Earth, we were trying to make sense out of the senselessness of war and the unrecoverable currency of youth.

We drank Everest beer long into the night and told stories like we were old friends. There was an easy, instant connection based on our military experiences and our shared attraction to the mountains. Soon, we were the last two in the dining room, and the exasperated lodge owner told us, in the overwhelmingly polite Sherpa way, that it was time for bed.

Kevin would be setting out in the morning with his group a few hours after I was scheduled to leave, and we would not see each other again before the climb. I said goodbye, we exchanged contact information, and that was it.

*　　*　　*

A day later, I stood on the summit of Island Peak. On that narrow cone of snow, my feet touched the earth at the same altitude at which jetliners and Air Force warplanes fly. But I didn't think about jetliners or warplanes, I only thought about how beautiful the view was and how hard I had worked to be there.

Before me, an endless vista of snowy peaks and glaciers stretched toward the jagged horizon. No other places on earth, except for the sea, are as overwhelming as the high mountains. Perhaps this is why we attribute such human qualities to these vast, inanimate landscapes. We look for God, after all, when we are at our most mortal, weak and impressed.

Then, as I looked down upon the distant villages I thought about something terrible, which I had tried so very hard to never think about again. But it was impossible to forget. I felt a familiar sadness, remembering why I was in this place at all. I had gone in search of wonders in these faraway places, hoping to discover some elusive truth that would allow me to return home and live an enlightened life. But, on that mountaintop, I learned the most common human experience was a life spent longing for the affection and opportunities I had waiting for me all along.

Krakauer was right about mountains and dreams because there's always another mountain to climb. Some other challenge left undone, which, you mistakenly think, is that one last obstacle before happiness. But the summit wasn't going to change me or reveal some hidden truth. It wasn't going to tell me what to do next. There was never any one thing I could achieve that would illuminate my path forward. My education was in the heavy price I found myself so willing to pay for such a meaningless achievement.

Later, I saw Kevin as I was descending from the summit. He was still on the way up with his father. They both looked tired but were determined to keep going. We stopped for a minute to shake hands, and I gave a brief account of my experience. Then we parted ways. I haven't seen Kevin since, and I've lost touch with him over the years. But I'll never forget meeting him. On the eve of the climb, the things I had wanted to leave behind ended up being my greatest comfort.

2012–2014: Telling Stories

It's Not Worth It

In the winter of 2011, I returned from the Himalayas, thin, bearded and brimming with excitement to begin the next phase of my life.

But war got in the way again.

The following year, while I pursued a master's degree at Northwestern's Medill School of Journalism, my rejuvenated fantasies of climbing mountains, traveling to the poles, and crossing deserts gave way to a need to return to war.

Why?

That's a question my friends, family and my girlfriend at the time often asked me.

Don't you want to move on and leave the wars behind?

What's the point anyway?

No one cares.

It's not worth it.

I never knew how to respond, incapable of explaining why I yearned to go back to war. Had I learned nothing from the Himalayas?

The truth was, returning to war was the path of least resistance when I was unsure of where to go next. Part of it, admittedly, was meeting the journalist James Foley, who had graduated a few classes ahead of me at Medill. While I was living in Chicago, James came back to Northwestern to give a talk about his 44 days as a prisoner in a Libyan jail during the 2001 civil war.

When I met James, he seemed vacant. His eyes never quite focused on mine, like he had been looking at the sun for too long. We had a chance to chat for a while about his work and the sense of purpose he gleaned from what he did, which we both agreed was practically impossible to recreate in civilian life.

The pull of conflict journalism is a lethal blend of both selfless purpose and totally selfish desires. It's a destructive behavior pattern that leaves you incapable of enjoying the banal details of life. Sadly, then, it's all too easy to miss out on the best days of your life when you've got your eyes permanently fixed on the horizon.

For people like James and me, comfort and predictability are our greatest fears. We would gladly risk losing a lifetime within safely repeatable circumstances to feel like we live fully today, and that our life means something because of it.

Meeting James was my fork in the road. It wasn't until later, long after James was dead, that I finally understood the dark side of the lives we'd chosen. Absent from my considerations as I embarked on this new career were the effects that such a vagabond existence of permanently living on the razor's edge of lethal danger had on those who loved me. Yes, we are all captains of our own destiny and we may choose to do what we wish with our lives and risk it all as we see fit. But there is always a cost. There always is. And love is not as perennial as you might assume when you test its boundaries so often.

Some suggested that I was an adrenaline junkie, and that normal life was failing to match the excitement and danger I had experienced as a military pilot. I didn't discount this argument and truly wondered if perhaps I just needed intermittent doses of extreme stress and danger to level out my personality.

But it was more than thrill seeking that drove me. As I tried to settle into Chicago and make new friends, I noticed in myself this cyclical worry that I was incapable of being happy. The chores of day-to-day living irritated me. Simple things like waiting in line at the grocery store, dealing with bills, or sitting in traffic—it all seemed unbearable. Meanwhile, I daydreamed of traveling to Syria. Clearly, my barometer for discomfort had been badly skewed along the way.

I would frequently disappear from my social circles for weeks on end. It was as if I had a cap to the amount of time I could spend around other people, and once I had hit that limit, I would withdraw and go into my own world, burying myself in my writing, working out, or planning for some new adventure.

Kelsey, my girlfriend at the time, was attending medical school in Florida, and we would often go months without seeing each other. We bickered frequently and there was a new distance in her voice when I mentioned marriage. I was losing her, I knew.

Nothing was going as I had hoped. I had left the military with an eye toward a newfound life of purpose and meaning. I wanted to rediscover dreams I had locked away after September 11, 2001, when going to war eclipsed all my other plans. Yet, a year after becoming a civilian I felt like an echo of the man I had once been.

I questioned my chosen career path and whether I had the talent to achieve it. I burned through my savings living in Chicago and took out student loans to pay rent. For the first time in my life I was beginning to worry about how to make ends meet.

I turned 30 halfway through my year at Medill and, as is the habit of many people at that age, fretted about where I was in life. I downplayed what I had accomplished in the military, cynically concluding that those experiences amounted to little in the civilian world other than lip-service expressions of gratitude and respect. Those friends of mine who had gone to the University of Florida were buying houses and starting families. They had achieved success and esteem in their careers. I judged myself according to them and felt like a failure. My father had been 28 when I was born. And yet, here I was at 30, taking loans to pay rent and buy groceries. The idea of marriage or being a father seemed impossibly distant and impractical. But, more than that, I felt like time was running out to live the adventurous life I'd always wanted.

*   *   *

As I neared graduation from Medill, conflict reporting seemed like the answer. I scoured the news for the most remote, forgotten conflicts. I thought about going to Mali to report on al-Qaeda terrorists in the Sahara. I considered a return to India and Nepal to report on Tibetan freedom fighters. I even thought about slipping into Syria to join some journalists I knew there at that time, including James Foley.

When I voiced these quixotic ideas to my parents and Kelsey, panic ensued. My transition from Air Force pilot to a wannabe writer had already caught everyone off guard. They were grateful, I think, that I had at least decided to start this new career by pursing a master's degree.

Around Christmas in 2012, just a week after I had finished my studies at Medill, I visited Sarasota. This was about the time I was seriously considering traveling to Mali and my parents thought it was a terrible idea. Islamist groups were at war in the country's north, spurring the French government to send in troops. The conflict was quickly escalating, even if it hardly made the news. It seemed like the kind of obscure opportunity I was looking for at the time to help launch my career. My parents, however, thought going to Mali was suicidal. We had a blowout argument about it over dinner at Bonefish Grill.

"You're going to get yourself killed for a story that no one cares about," my dad said.

"But people are suffering, Dad," I countered, dutifully falling back on altruism to defend a bad idea. "They deserve to have their story told."

"Nolan, look around," my dad replied. He spoke deliberately. "No one here cares about Mali. Even if you wrote the most incredible stories in the history of journalism, nothing would change that. Is that worth dying for?"

I got mad, and we got into it. My mom shut down and was silent the whole time. I argued that good people were suffering while most of us continue on, oblivious to the darkness that exists around the world. My reasoning was impassioned, but honestly, my dad was right. Distant wars in places that few Americans have ever visited, much less heard of, don't rank highly among their daily concerns. Still, it's not easy to have your dad tell you that your budding life's passion is irrelevant.

What eluded me at the time, however, was the disproportionate ratio between my dad's love for me and his empathy for people in those faraway lands. No story, no foreign war, no human tragedy—no matter its scale—would ever be worth risking his son's life. Hidden under the shroud of my selfish indignity, I failed to understand that my dad was just worried about me. For him, the danger of me going to the war zone in Mali seemed absurd when weighed against the likely impact my stories would have.

*   *   *

Despite my steadfast convictions, my career as a war correspondent got off to a lethargic start. After graduating from Medill, I promptly began applying for jobs. I had to, of course, because the payment schedule for my student loans kicked in right away. I'd naïvely expected that my background as an Air Force pilot and my high marks at Medill would make me immediately competitive for a job at a major outlet. I wasn't necessarily gunning for the front page of the *New York Times* right away, but I thought that with two master's degrees to my name and my military background I could at least get my foot in the door somewhere.

Well, reality was like a Mike Tyson punch to the gut. Six months of fruitless job searches later, despite scoring the occasional freelance gig to scrape by on my bills, I had gone nowhere. Chicago became too expensive, so, while I continued to send out job applications, I decided to move to Key West to spend the summer finishing a novel I was working on at the time. Again, I pulled the ejection handle on my life—I sold off most of my things, threw what was left in storage and rented a car for the long drive down to Florida.

In Key West, I lived above a Lebanese restaurant in a rented room with a shared bathroom. I didn't have a car, just a bicycle I had bought from Target on the way into town. It was a humbling moment, to put it mildly, with quite a few mornings spent looking at myself in the mirror, wondering what the fuck I had done with my life.

Once, I'd felt like Captain America. A hero to my friends and family. Now, I was living in a hovel in Key West, trying not to listen through the thin walls as a prostitute entertained clients next door while the smell of weed and other things wafted under the door jamb.

I finished the novel, but it was roundly and predictably rejected by publishers. Meanwhile, my job search had been equally as fruitless. Still, I wasn't ready to quit. I would rather live this way, I obstinately if desperately decided, than waste what I considered to be my gifts. I was quickly becoming a martyr to my career choice.

In the Air Force my hard work had always translated into opportunities and success. I studied hard at the Academy, and I earned a pilot training slot and a scholarship for graduate school in Paris. I worked hard in pilot training, and I was selected for supersonic T-38 fighter trainers. As a pilot, I trained countless hours for the honor of flying combat missions.

Now, I couldn't catch a break. As the rejection letters piled up I watched my savings trickle to nothing, To make ends meet, in Key West I worked as a bartender and a personal trainer. In the darkest days, I even applied to be a truck driver and a security guard at K–Mart. And just to round things out, around that time Kelsey and I finally broke up. We'd been together more than four years, and there were a lot of things said when we split. But one thing stood out more than any other.

"I thought your trip to the Himalayas would change you," she said. "But nothing changed."

*   *   *

At the end of that summer in Key West my younger brother Drew came with some friends to visit me for a long weekend. Drew was an Air Force captain then, and he was preparing for his second deployment to Afghanistan as the mission commander of a classified National Reconnaissance Office (NRO) operation.

The NRO is the top-secret intelligence agency in charge of the nation's spy satellites and other airborne reconnaissance platforms. Drew couldn't tell me much, or anything really, about what he would be doing in Afghanistan (he still can't), but he did say he'd be working out of Bagram Air Base, just north of Kabul.

"You should try to get over to Afghanistan while I'm there," Drew casually suggested as we sipped on rumrunners and watched the sunset to the background din of Jimmy Buffett covers at a seaside tiki bar. It was a casual remark that I didn't take all that seriously at the time. We were in Key West, after all, and I chalked up most of what was said to the booze. Nevertheless, the idea of going back to Afghanistan stuck. This could be my ticket, I believed the more I thought about it. The story about two brothers reuniting in a war zone, one of whom was returning as a witness to a war in which he had previously been a combatant. If I could pull it off, surely that would launch my career. Surely.

So after Drew and my friends departed, I got to work on finding a way to Afghanistan. From within the little hovel off Duval Street that was my home, I waded into the morass of applying to NATO for an embedded journalism slot. This was a complicated process for a journalist working for a major outlet, and a true ordeal for what I was at that time—an unemployed novice with close to zero professional connections. Not only would I have to get NATO to sign off on the embed and connect me with a unit willing to host me, but I would also have to convince a news outlet to give me credentials and guarantee to publish my work.

I wouldn't be able to embed with Drew's unit. His work was too sensitive for journalists to observe. So my plan was to embed with a US combat unit in RC East (the eastern section of the war zone), which would allow me to transit through Bagram on the way out to one of the more remote forward operating bases. That was my best chance to see Drew.

I sent story pitches to all the major outlets. And my luck was nothing if not consistent—no one was interested. No one. My initial enthusiasm quickly deflated when I realized that I had two major strikes against me: (1) Afghanistan was a back-page story, and (2) I was an unknown, unproven journalist.

The idea of actually making money from the trip wasn't even a consideration at this point. At best, I could offset a portion of the expenses to get to Afghanistan and rent body armor. But the biggest challenge remained obtaining credentials. NATO and the US military wouldn't allow a freelance journalist to embed with their forces unless a legitimate media outlet guaranteed to publish that journalist's stories. It was a reasonable demand, I must admit, given the time and money the military devotes to transporting, housing, and protecting embedded journalists. (Later on, my time on the front lines in Ukraine imparted a healthy appreciation for the US military's embedded journalism operation.) If the US military was going to fly a journalist around the combat theater over the span of a few weeks, then they wanted to make damn sure that journalist's stories were actually going to be published.

The bottom line was that I had to find an outlet willing to give me credentials—and quickly. Drew was set to deploy at the end of the summer and would be in Afghanistan until about Christmas. The clock was ticking. After the Fourth of July holiday I decided to leave Key West, and took a job at a weekly newspaper back in my hometown called the *Sarasota Observer*. It was a way to pay the bills. It was also, as I look back on that time now, an invaluable way to hone my skills as a journalist. I reported on County Commission and School Board meetings, covering hot topics like beach parking permits, school lunches and noise ordinances. Not quite the earth-shattering stuff I had envisioned for myself, but cranking out one story a day on topics that hardly interested me developed my craft in a way that writing freelance features over the easygoing span of a few months never did.

I was a bit snotty about it at the time, I'm sorry to say, but the daily beat of small-town, shoe-leather journalism truly was a better education in writing and reporting than any master's degree. Those months at the *Sarasota Observer* were the most formative of my career, and I'm grateful for them.

Ultimately, I was able to convince a friend of mine at United Press International to write me a letter of accreditation and a guarantee to publish my stories from Afghanistan. The catch was they weren't going to pay me. Not for airfare, body armor, life insurance, or the visa. Nothing. In fact, they weren't even going to pay for my stories. Basically, I was going into a war zone on my own dime to write stories pro bono. But by that point I didn't care. I just wanted a way to get to Afghanistan. My new life was floundering, and I needed to do something drastic. So I dumped my savings, sold my triathlon bike and old guitar, and started a crowd-funding campaign on the internet. I was able to scrape together enough cash for a plane ticket to Afghanistan and body armor.

With my letter of accreditation from UPI in hand, NATO promptly approved me for an embedded assignment with the US Army's 10th Mountain Division. Graciously, my boss at the *Sarasota Observer*—Matt Walsh, whose son was an active duty Marine at the time—said my job would be waiting for me when I got home. Thus, at the end of November 2013, with only a few weeks left before Drew was supposed to return home, I departed Miami International Airport on my way to Afghanistan.

Brothers in Arms

Bagram Air Base, Afghanistan
November 2013

It's time to say goodbye.

We both get out of the truck and circle around back to give each other a hug. It's hard to see Drew's face in the dark—Bagram Air Base is blacked out as a defense against Taliban rocket and mortar attacks. But I can see my brother's silhouette and hear his voice.

We embrace. The hug is a little tighter, and it lasts a little longer than usual.

Drew pulls back and places both hands on my shoulders like he's holding me in place, making sure his words find their mark.

"Don't be a hero," he says.

He starts to say something else, but then he stops, and that's when I notice that he's crying.

"I've seen a lot of people get hurt out there," he says at last. "Be safe."

I tell him I will, feeling a wave of guilt wash over me for some reason as we part ways.

That night I load onto a CH-47 Chinook helicopter for a flight out to a forward operating base in Khost Province near the Afghanistan-Pakistan border. En route, we take fire and the door gunner shoots back. The gun is loud inside the cabin and the muzzle flashes leave yellow spots in my night-vision adjusted eyes. It's a dark night and the enemy is probably just blindly shooting at the rotor noise. We probably aren't in any real danger. Still, I'm terrified.

*　　*　　*

I had arrived in Kabul, Afghanistan's capital, on the afternoon of the previous day. On the flight in from Dubai, I sipped on a Diet Coke and listened to my iPod. Out the window I recognized the terrain from combat missions. On my first arrival in Afghanistan several years earlier, an Army chaplain had recited the poem "Invictus" as the C-17 cargo plane spiraled to a blacked-out landing to avoid surface-to-air missiles. The chaplain intoned, "Out of the night that covers me, Black as the pit from pole to pole, I thank whatever gods may be for my unconquerable soul..."

This time, I had to fold up my tray table.

"Enjoy your stay in Kabul," the flight attendant said.

My stay in Kabul lasted just the one night. Then I loaded onto an Air Force C-130 with a group of US Army troops for the short flight up to Bagram Air Base, an old Soviet facility that became NATO's hub in northern Afghanistan.

At the Bagram passenger terminal I met my liaison, an Army master sergeant with a high and tight haircut, scars on his face, and a lot of patches on his uniform. He wasn't exactly thrilled to be shepherding a journalist around, although he was polite about it. I would be leaving on a Chinook for a FOB near the Pakistan border that night, the soldier explained, and I had the day free. I said I needed to make a stop at the old Russian control tower. When I told him why, a broad smile crept over the master sergeant's weathered face, smoothing his furled brow.

"Too easy," he said.

Minutes later, I was sitting on a picnic table beside the battle-scarred control tower when a lone figure in combat fatigues rounded the corner a few hundred yards away. I instantly recognized Drew's smile even though he wore a brown beanie and dark sunglasses and was dressed in the same uniform as everyone else. But it just didn't seem real, not even after we hugged and he was standing right there in front of me.

Suddenly, I felt it all.

A pebble under my shoe as I shifted my balance from the hug. A cold wind at my neck; the smell of dust in the air. The lower flanks of the faraway Hindu Kush mountains, colored purple by the distance. As if it all hadn't been there a moment ago. Or, I hadn't.

Seeing Drew made the here and now my reality. There was nothing left of me in some other place, safely distant from the war. The notion that I was truly back in Afghanistan, with the shadowy enemy lurking somewhere out there—well, it had just seemed like a dream. Too disconnected from the life I had been living to be true. But seeing Drew shattered that protective shield of disbelief.

"I can't believe you're here," Drew said.

Yes, I was really there.

And then I felt something that had never even crossed my mind during all the months of planning for my embedded journalism assignment. Fear. It wasn't like I had ignored the risks of coming back to this place. I knew I wasn't immune to its dangers. Still, I must admit that while planning this trip from the comfort of my apartment in Sarasota, the war had failed to inspire any real fear. My budding civilian life had divorced me from war's realities. But reuniting with Drew in Afghanistan made me feel naked, exposed, and in danger. If my brother was there, then all of me was there, too. The war felt very real again.

Later, my brother and I smoked Cuban cigars, which I had smuggled in, as we watched F–16s take off en route to combat. The afterburners glowed purple in the night.

"Epic," was a word we threw around a lot that night.

* * *

I was the first person in my family to hold Drew after he was born. Although I was only four years old, I remember when the doctor took the Transformers toy out of my hand before placing my infant brother in my arms.

Decades later, Drew attended the US Air Force Academy as I had. He was there at my graduation, and four years later I read the oath at Drew's commissioning ceremony. We always felt like we had a special bond because of that shared experience. I thought about those memories in the moments after Drew and I parted ways that night at Bagram. I also wondered if one of us would have to carry the memory of seeing his brother for the last time.

This might sound dark to those of you who have never been in combat or sent a loved one off to war, but when I had hugged Drew goodbye before he left for Afghanistan, four months prior to our meeting at Bagram, I found myself working to emblazon that memory in my mind. Instinctively, I worried it could be the last time I ever saw him.

I did something similar before I left for Afghanistan myself, making each farewell a complete one, with nothing left unsaid. The specter of my death loomed over every goodbye. This might be how they remember me forever, I kept telling myself, and I considered how poetically perfect each farewell would be if I did die in Afghanistan. It would be tragic, yes, but how rare is it to say goodbye to everyone in your life? Anyway, like I said, unless you've sent someone off to war or gone yourself this all might seem a bit dramatic. But that's how I felt, and I imagine I'm not only one who's had those thoughts.

War does that; it makes you see things a little differently. It reminds you that everything is temporary, and you're never able to shake this feeling that everything you do in a war zone you might be doing for the last time.

It also evokes one word, over and over again in your mind—*why*.

Why am I here?

Why is the enemy fighting?

Why can't we just go home?

They asked why when we went to the Academy, too. Why not go to an Ivy League school and make more money? Why not go to the University of Florida and have fun? Why go to a school where they yell at you and make you march on Saturdays?

When Drew volunteered for his second deployment to Afghanistan, there were many who asked him, "Why?"

Why put your life on the line when someone else could easily go and do it for you?

Those of us who volunteered for military service in the wake of 9/11 are now at the tail end of young adulthood. Many of us have moved on to new endeavors. Some have decided to remain in the military and will comprise the next generation of battle-tested American military leaders. They will likely be fighting the same enemy for the rest of their careers, and lives.

There's a noble ideal, I think, which motivated most of us who served after 9/11. Yet it's easy to be jaded after so many years of war. I remember the conversations I had with the older pilots during my first deployment to Afghanistan. They explained to me how some of the Taliban commanders we were going after were the same militants they had successfully captured years ago. The enemy soldiers would spend a year or two in some prison, and then be released, inevitably making their way back to the battlefield.

"It's hard not to feel like my career has been a gigantic waste of time," I remember a lieutenant colonel telling me on the walk to dinner at Bagram Air Base one night.

"I've deployed eight times," he said. "I've missed my kids growing up, I've missed a decade with my wife. For what? Seriously, what the fuck have we done here?"

Those words stuck with me, particularly since it was my first deployment and I was already mesmerized by the epic experience of going to war. And like most FNGs—"fucking new guys," as we were delicately called—for me the experience was a rite of passage, somehow validating my place among all those who had stepped up and fought for our country after 9/11. Consequently, the cynicism of the older pilots was particularly deflating. I began to suspect that this war was pointless and unwinnable. Above all, it was hard to imagine what victory, or peace, would look like.

So why go?

"There are people still fighting over there," my brother explained. "I'd feel like I wasn't doing my job if I didn't do something to help out the war-fighters."

Into the Storm

My short stint as a war reporter in Afghanistan changed nothing. Shortly after my return I went right back to writing stories about School Board meetings for the *Sarasota Observer*. I had two options. First, I could be comfortable where I was, with what I was doing. And truly, working and living in Sarasota, Florida was no great burden to bear. Or, once again, I could sell whatever I didn't need, throw the rest in storage, and set off for another war. It really wasn't a choice at all. By July 2014, the bags were packed. I just didn't know where to go.

At that time, the war in Gaza was in full force as was the war in Ukraine. I had some friends in Israel who offered to set me up with a place to stay and get me access to the military and the front lines. Yet, although I disagreed with the anti-Israel slant of much of the media coverage, the Gaza conflict was squarely under the media's microscope. I was unsure how I could make a mark doing anything noteworthy in a war inundated with so many other journalists.

The war in Ukraine, on the other hand, was a mystery. The details emerging from that conflict were murky, contradictory, and confusing. I had no clear picture of what was actually happening on the ground.

Still, there were reports of tank battles and heavy artillery. Russian surface-to-air missiles were shooting down Ukrainian warplanes every week, it seemed. Heavy fighting, a real war. And it all, even from afar, felt like a secret.

An act of mass murder ultimately tipped the balance in favor of me going to Ukraine. When a Russian surface-to-air missile shot down Malaysia Airlines Flight 17 that July, killing all 298 people on board, I made up my mind. I would somehow find my way to the front lines in eastern Ukraine and tell the world the truth about a forgotten war. Without enough money to get there on my own, I was grateful when Drew stepped in and bought me a one-way ticket to Kyiv.

"Whatever happens, just don't die," he told me. "Mom and Dad would never forgive me."

*　　*　　*

My parents drove me from Sarasota to Tampa International Airport at 5 a.m. to catch my 7 a.m. flight to New York. From there I would fly to Amsterdam and then on to Kyiv, the capital of Ukraine.

It was a strained car ride that July morning. To break the tension, every so often Mom would ask some perfunctory question, like if I had packed enough clothes or if I needed any snacks for the plane ride. She was nervous and uncertain how to behave in the lead-up to this goodbye.

As we drove north on I-75 periodic lightning illuminated the tropical summer sky, highlighting the outlines of the tall thunderheads looming like mountains over the flat peninsula. In the pre-dawn dark the sounds of the tires on the road and air slipping past the windows seemed amplified. So, too, was the awkward silence in the car that Mom was determined to interrupt.

"So, do you have a place to stay when you arrive?" she asked.

"I have it all worked out."

"What about money?"

"I can use ATMs, Mom."

"How long do you think you'll be gone?"

"Just a couple weeks."

"And you won't be anywhere near the fighting, right?"

"Right."

"You promise?"

"Yes, Mom. Ukraine is huge. It's about the same distance from Kyiv to the front lines as it is from Sarasota to Atlanta. I won't be in any danger."

She knew I was only saying what she wanted to hear, but somehow my halfhearted white lies seemed to make her feel a little better. I could tell she was desperate for a way to be involved.

Of course, there's no instruction manual on how to send your son off to war. Especially as a conflict journalist. My parents were worried, and I don't blame them. They were afraid because they had no way to imagine where I would be going. For them, Ukraine was a blank spot on the map. A place that had been the forbidden heart of America's enemy—the Soviet Union—for most of their lives. There was no corollary in their own lives upon which they could construct a mental image of where I was going. And we often forget to include the ordinary details when we rely wholly on imagination.

"Try to call us every now and then," Mom said.

"Of course, Mom. You have nothing to worry about."

She said nothing.

Dad remained silent for most of the drive, even as Mom continued to throw out questions at intervals as random as the occasional downpour through which we drove. As we crossed the Sunshine Skyway Bridge spanning Tampa Bay, the blinking red lights at the top of the twin cable-support columns glowed through the low clouds in a softly distorted way. It reminded me of the way explosions look in night-vision goggles.

As we turned off the interstate into the airport entrance, my father spoke.

"Promise me you won't go near the fighting," he said.

"I promise I'll be careful."

"You're not invincible," he said, his eyes fixed on the road ahead. "Remember, this isn't your war. It's not worth dying for."

"I know." I lied.

We parked at the curb outside departures. All three of us got out to say our goodbyes and take a few smiling photos. Mom kept a hand on my shoulder as I unloaded my hiking rucksack from the trunk and heaved it onto my back. I hugged her and she kept telling me to be careful and to call her often.

"You'll be back in a few weeks, right?" she asked again.

"Yes. Definitely not longer than a month."

She said she loved me and hugged me one last time, pressing the side of her face into my chest.

I turned to Dad and he hugged me so hard I lost balance and staggered a bit to stay standing straight. When I pulled away I noticed his eyes were full of tears.

"I'm so tired of sending my sons off to war," he said.

James Foley

War is murder. War is survival.
War is suffering. War is funny.
War is chaos and noise and fear. War is boring.
War is hate. War is love.
War is hell. War is glorious.
War is all these things, because above all war is human.

And unless brave men and women like James Foley venture into war to tell us the truth about what is happening there, both the ugly and the beautiful parts of it, then the people who suffer and fight in wars will have no voice.

People like James are the only obstacle to war becoming the worst thing it can be—forgotten.

* * *

I heard the news of James's murder on the eve of my first trip to eastern Ukraine's war zone in August 2014. I was steeling myself for combat, and the sad news made the risks seem a hell of a lot more real. And the way his death affected his parents, well, it was just a little too easy for my mind's eye to replace his sobbing parents on TV with my own. I was able to clearly imagine how my death in a war zone would play out after seeing the reactions to his.

James and I had a lot in common, after all.

We're both graduates of the master's program at the Medill School of Journalism. James was a couple years ahead of me but we had the same teachers, many of whom reached out to me after James died, reminding me to be careful.

"Like you, he used to send me his stories from the front," one of my Medill professors wrote. "Like you, he had one fuck of a lot of guts! He was an outstanding guy, and his murder has just ripped me apart."

James and I both also had careers prior to pursuing journalism. He had been an elementary school teacher before he attended Medill in his 30s. James never served in the military, but his brother Michael was in the Air Force.

"I don't even know how a human being can even have that fierce and intense hate for someone else," Michael said, speaking about his brother's murderers in an interview with Katie Couric. "I don't even understand where that type of hate comes from."

Reading those words, watching the interview—it didn't take too much effort to imagine Drew saying those things about me. It made me sick to think about. It also made me consider the consequences of my military background if I were ever kidnapped in a war zone.

According to news reports, ISIS guards singled out James for especially brutal treatment when they discovered through a Facebook search that he had a brother in the US military.

"He became the whipping boy of the jailers, but he remained implacable," recalled French journalist Nicolas Henin, who was imprisoned with Foley.

Looking back, a chill goes down my spine as I remember passing though pro-Russian separatist checkpoints near Donetsk and the close calls I had. I can't help but wonder, "What the fuck was I thinking?"

* * *

The news of James's murder prompted a panicked flood of messages from friends and family who knew I was in Ukraine to report on the war. Many of the notes included something to the effect of, "No story is worth dying for."

And they're completely right. Even James thought so.

"Because it's not worth your life," James said when he spoke about his time in Libya to Medill students in 2011. "It's not worth seeing your mother, father, brother, and sister bawling. You're worrying about your grandmother dying because you're in prison. It's not worth these things. It's not worth your life no matter what romantic ideal you have, no matter what ethic you think you have. It's never worth that."

I completely agree with James. And yet, I still went to eastern Ukraine. And Afghanistan. And Iraq. Again and again and again.

There is something mysterious that happens to a war correspondent in a war zone. It's the thing that draws us to these dangerous places, even though we know that no story is worth the risk. And I suspect, although I could never speak for him, this is one reason why James went back to the Middle East after his ordeal in Libya.

What happens is you start to care. The story and the people who comprise it are no longer separate, distinguishable things. They merge, and deciding whether a story is "worth it" becomes a lot more complicated.

History rarely hinges on one news story. So, when judged soberly, no one story is ever worth dying for. It's easy, then, to dismiss the value of another trip to the front lines when the currency is page views. It becomes much murkier when weighing friendship and affection. That's because war is a fusion of the best and worst in people. From far away its ugliness makes war abhorrent. But from up close it's the humanity of war that makes it addictive. Every war story becomes about the people in it. And it's really, really hard to report on a war and not take a side. You see the suffering and start to believe things are so bad because no one is paying attention. You begin to think that the right words or the perfect photo could spur those back home to give a damn.

Well, the truth is most people back home don't care. And they probably never will. Yet, you see firsthand how your presence affects the people around you. When I look into the eyes of a friend in Ukraine, or a 19-year-old American soldier in Afghanistan, and my willingness to tell his or her story is the one tenuous filament left suspending hope from sinking into despair… that's when decisions happen that words alone can't explain.

That's when a story becomes "worth it."

There's something else, too, which I'd be remiss if I didn't admit. Yes, James's murder horrified me. But it also pissed me off. I won't let scum like ISIS be the ones who write history—first draft or not. And I won't let the world forget the good people who stood up for what was right when the world was at its worst.

James was one of those people, and I won't forget his story.

2014–2015: A Forgotten War

This Isn't My War

In February 2014, Ukrainian protesters had braved snipers on Kyiv's central square during a revolution to overthrow Viktor Yanukovych, the country's pro-Russian president. It was a national triumph, proclaiming the country's desire for a pro-European future, but the revolution's final days had been murderous. The Berkut special police force under Yanukovych's command launched a brutal crackdown. Ultimately, about 100 protesters died in the revolution's closing days, many due to snipers.

Days after Yanukovych's ouster, Russian troops appeared across Crimea, deploying from their country's naval base in the city of Sevastopol. Under the watchful gaze of these patchless Russian special forces troops—the "little green men," as they're now known—Crimean officials held a farcical referendum to join the Russian Federation that March.

The war began on April 6, 2014, when Russian security agents and Spetsnaz (Special Forces) troops, using Russia's hybrid warfare playbook, engineered an uprising, which spawned two Russian-backed territories in eastern Ukraine's Donbas region—the Donetsk People's Republic, or DNR, and the Luhansk People's Republic, or LNR.

Through propaganda, Russia painted its 2014 seizure of Crimea and the ensuing conflict in the Donbas as grassroots uprisings created and led by disaffected Russian-speaking Ukrainians who believed the new government in Kyiv was the illegitimate product of a CIA-orchestrated putsch. That was all a lie. The war remains, and always has been, a Russian invasion.

The situation was dire in the summer of 2014. Officials advised citizens in Kyiv to use the city's metro in case of a Russian aerial bombardment or artillery blitz. Spray-painted signs on the sides of buildings pointing to the nearest bomb shelter became ubiquitous sights in cities across Ukraine. A combined force of pro-Russian separatists and Russian regulars was on the march in eastern Ukraine, and there were worries then that the country could be split in two. For its part, Ukraine's regular army had been decimated by decades of corruption and was only able to field 6,000 combat-ready soldiers at that time.

With Ukraine's regular army on its heels, everyday Ukrainians filled the ranks of irregular, civilian combat units. They headed out to the country's east, where they faced Russian tanks, artillery, and the Kremlin's regular troops in a land war to preserve their country's sovereignty. At the same time, legions of volunteers collected and delivered supplies to support the front-line troops—often at great risk.

It was a grassroots war effort, underscoring a widespread attitude of self-reliance among Ukrainian citizens who were unwilling to wait for the government to act in a moment of crisis. By July of 2014, Ukraine's ragtag armed forces (the "Bad News Bears" of war, as I call them) had retaken 23 out of the 36 districts previously under combined Russian-separatist control. With its troops on the march, it looked, briefly, like Kyiv might be able to take back all the territory it had previously lost to Russia's proxies.

In August, however, Russia sent in thousands of its own troops and massive amounts of weaponry and military hardware. The conflict escalated to tank battles, heavy artillery barrages, and rocket attacks. A sack on the port city of Mariupol, home to half a million people, looked imminent.

The stakes were dire. Should Mariupol fall, Moscow would gain a virtually unimpeded land corridor along the Sea of Azov coastline, connecting mainland Russian territory to the Crimean Peninsula.

Thus, in the waning days of August 2014, the Ukrainian soldiers sent to defend Mariupol were ready for a bloodbath. In the city, civilians were similarly resigned, throwing around words like "Grozny" and "Stalingrad." No one took events at that time lightly. In fact, it felt like things were spiraling rapidly out of control.

* * *

Kyiv, Ukraine
September 2, 2014

The war is always there, but it isn't mine. Stepping off the train in Kyiv, walking into the crowd, I feel everyone swirling around me at a half-beat faster rhythm than my own. Young women stroll by indifferently; young men bump into my shoulder in a hurry somewhere.

I'm stuck in another place, at another speed, living within. My mind is locked to Semyonovka.

I was there the day before, near the war's front lines. Whole neighborhoods flattened by artillery. Trees stripped bare of leaves and branches by the blasts. An old woman with her arms folded stood on a street corner, framed by the ruined leftovers of her hometown.

"I have nowhere else to go," she said, shrugging her shoulders.

An old man with leather-skinned hands sat on a bench down the street, the wall behind him speckle-scarred by shrapnel. He looked at me suspiciously.

"Nothing you write will change anything here," he said, pointing down the cratered road with an upturned hand.

At a street corner a few blocks away a woman and child waited for a bus to take them away from this wasteland. Behind them workers rebuilt the destroyed bus station.

A woman and child wait for a ride out of the war-torn town of Semyonovka in eastern Ukraine in July 2014. The most important part of any war story is neither the clash of armies nor the perversion of politics—it's the tragedy of life interrupted.

The fighting has stopped in Semyonovka, but the war is always there. It could come back, but no one knows.

A few hours by train and I'm back in Kyiv. Far enough from the war to make it feel like fiction, but there are subtle signs of it here.

Blue and yellow ribbons on women's purses. Soldiers with Kalashnikovs standing around Kyiv's central square, the Maidan. Ukrainian flags hanging out windows and trailing from the radio antennas of cars. Posters on Khreshchatyk Avenue asking Ukrainians to support their troops. I go to dinner and the restaurant is giving a portion of its revenue to support wounded soldiers. But the war here is a cause, a rallying cry, not a real war. It's a reason to be proud and wave the flag and debate politics and somberly shake one's head at the sad news coming from the front every day. But it's not a real war, even though it's always there. Just like back home. People take a minute to thank the troops, and then life goes on. The troops, though, are never done. They can't move on because wars never end for those who fight them.

The real war touches Kyiv lightly, like a feather. It's easy to miss if you don't look for it or don't want to.

There, at the entrance to the train station, a young man in uniform with his military rucksack is kissing his girlfriend goodbye. He holds her face with both his hands, controlling for a second longer the only thing he can. Bullet holes are still in trees and street signs at the top of Institutskaya Street near the Maidan, where Berkut riot police thugs and snipers gunned down protesters in February. Now the place is covered in flowers and tourists march past.

In the metro a young woman listens to music on her iPhone, and students laugh and talk. An old woman sits on the bench, a cane in one hand and a plastic bag full of something down between her feet. What her life must have been like—millions dead in Ukraine during the famine of 1932 to 1933, hundreds of thousands killed during Stalin's purges from 1934 to 1940, about seven million Ukrainians killed during World War II, and then a half-century of Soviet rule. She stares forward, emotionless. Maybe she's thinking about her wars, maybe she's thinking about what to make for dinner.

After Semyonovka I stay in Kyiv for a few weeks. I keep writing. I want to go back to the front, but there's talk now of the separatists kidnapping and murdering foreigners. I think about my friend James Foley, and I remember how brave he was with the knife to his throat. I think about what I've already seen in Afghanistan and Iraq. I've had friends die in those wars, too. I read news that Chechens are fighting with the separatists in eastern Ukraine. A friend offers me a ride to Donetsk. Fuck that.

And then Russia invades southeastern Ukraine and there's talk of a siege on Mariupol. I reflexively buy a train ticket for tomorrow and make a hotel reservation.

*   *   *

It's almost time to go catch the train, and I'm scared. What if I go and it spirals out of control? What if it ends up like Semyonovka?

The train leaves at five, and I have some time. I think of a lot of reasons not to go. I leave myself a way out, and it doesn't seem so real.

I lie down on my bed and read a book. I get comfortable and decide I'm not going. Then I wonder why I'm here, and what it's all worth if I don't go. I decide I'm going. Not much time left now, so I pack my bag in a hurry. Everything ready and I open the door to leave. I stop. I flash forward to flashing back to this moment as a memory. I wonder if I'll regret this decision, this one right now, to go to Mariupol. What if the separatists break through the lines? What if I can't get out and I'm kidnapped? I think about James in the orange jumpsuit.

I close the door and put my bag down. I'm staying.

The war is still there, but this isn't my war. It can't be worth it to leave Kyiv and go to the fighting. Not enough people read my stories for them to make a difference, and even if they did, what do I owe Ukraine anyway? It's a sunny, late summer day in Kyiv and there are cafés where I can work and write, streets to wander and explore, and bars to visit at night to drink beer and talk politics with friends.

But then, without thinking, I pick up my bag and I'm out the door. Walking to the metro station like I'm skiing down a hill, willfully giving myself to gravity, constantly gathering momentum. It's easier to keep going this way than to turn back around. I'm off the metro, back into the train station. I'm moving at the right speed now. I've been cured of the war by the few weeks in Kyiv.

Soon I'm on the train and pulling away. The train picks up speed, the world blurs by but I'm slowing down inside. That familiar feeling of sliding into a war zone returns. My senses pick up. There's a constant, inescapable sense of dread. My stomach rumbles, but I'm not hungry. I wanted to write on the train ride, but that hunger is gone too.

The train goes into the night and south toward the war.

I think back to what my dad told me: "Remember, this isn't your war."

He's right, this isn't my war. But I'm still drawn to it like it's my own. Is it just because it's there? Is it because I want it to be mine? I already have my own war, after all. But maybe when you have one war you have them all.

No matter now. I'm on a train heading back to war, and I can't get off. And when I'm back in it, the war won't care whether it's mine or not. And neither will I.

*   *   *

Mariupol, Ukraine
September 3, 2014

Despite the fact that the combined Russian-separatist army is only 20 to 30 kilometers outside the city, life here seems unaffected. People were at the beach today, enjoying the late summer sun. Children were in school, and rail and aviation routes are still open. The hotel I'm at offers the clearest sign of what may be about to happen. The place is swarming with journalists from around the world. At the bar they swap stories from Iraq, Afghanistan, Sudan, Congo...

This is all amid the backdrop of Ukrainian troops digging in on the outskirts of town for what looks to be a tough fight against Russia's so-called separatist army, which may include as many as 1,000 Russian regular troops, according to NATO.

So tonight I'm sitting at a café on the Sea of Azov, listening to awful American cover songs on the radio as I plan interviews for tomorrow, as well as my escape plan if things spiral out of control.

It's a quiet, clear night. A steady sea breeze rocks the trees, and the lights of different towns along the coast twinkle in the clear air, just like the stars in the dark sky above.

As I sip my second beer of the evening (what else is there to do under the circumstances?), I write down my impressions of today and scan the news online for updates.

It all reminds me of my childhood in Florida, and my memories of when a hurricane was on the horizon. Often the days leading up to a hurricane are beautiful and clear, with a slight, steady breeze—just like tonight in Mariupol. The weather portends nothing of the tempest just over the horizon. But the calm and the peace seem so finite and precious with the knowledge of what is to come.

It's bizarre to scroll through my Facebook feed to see life going on back home, unaffected by all of this. I know, of course, that this isn't America's war and few people back home have personal connections to this place or the people in it. But when I see the fear in the look of the woman working the desk of the hotel, or on the faces of the young soldiers getting off the train today and being trucked to the trenches on the outskirts of the city, I can't help but think people back home should care more about all of this.

At a minimum, I think, our leaders should understand what may be about to happen here. And they should be willing to do something about it. Or maybe I've just gotten too caught up in this, caring too much about a conflict that has little to do with my life back home.

But the most lasting, important impression of today is that there are a lot of normal, good people here who want nothing more than to just go about their lives in peace. They don't have the option, like I do, to just pack up and leave. This is their home and where they will likely stay no matter the outcome of the next few days. And they go to sleep tonight not knowing what tomorrow will bring.

* * *

Mariupol, Ukraine
September 4, 2014

I'm at a Georgian restaurant on a hilltop at the edge of Mariupol. The sky is clear and the stars are out. I have one hand wrapped around my beer, which I sip often.

Out in the distance, toward the dark void in the direction of Donetsk, there is a storm. Flashes of light reveal stop-motion images of the blackened horizon. The percussive thuds roll in seconds later, out of synch with the light show like the delay between lightning and thunder in a Florida summer squall. But this is not a storm of wind and rain. It is one of fire and steel.

Out there, a battle rages. Artillery, rockets, and mortars explode. Soldiers are killing and dying. While I'm here, at my perch, on the balcony of an open-air restaurant, safely cocooned by the miles, casually sipping on a beer. I have a front-row seat to the grimmest of contests.

An evening sea breeze has cooled the warm summer day. It's a dark, quarter-moon night, and the sky is clear. The mood at this restaurant is as dark as the night. There are no lovers on dates, no children running around their parents' table misbehaving. Through the glass walls of the restaurant, I can see servers sitting in silent rapture before television screens on which news reports speak of the war and a possible cease-fire.

The terrace is mostly empty, save for some old men sitting outside with me. They sip their vodka or beer as the rumble of the faraway battle washes over us like a wave calmly spilling itself on a beach.

I order another beer, and as the alcohol catches up I feel like the world is closing in on my thoughts. Below me, rows of city lights, within which half a million people are nervously hunkered down in their homes, not knowing if they will wake up tomorrow morning to the sound of Russian tank treads clanking down the street. I find myself thinking about the same possibility, realizing, quite suddenly and soberly, that I would have no idea what to do in such a situation.

I look down from my elevated perch. I imagine the life stories playing out behind each twinkling city light. What do parents say to their children in such a moment? What comforts do lovers find in each other's embrace? Would those who were alive for the Nazi and Soviet invasions be reliving memories and emotions, which they had tried so very hard to forget?

From here the war is just lightning and thunder. The people in its inevitable path are nothing more to me than distant city lights. I watch, out there in the distance, a real battle while I enjoy a beer and the night breeze lapping at my neck. I'm a spectator to the destruction of men while distance safely cocoons me. A silent observer, like a god on Mount Olympus. Or, like an Air Force pilot orbiting high above the battlefields of Iraq and Afghanistan, disconnected from the danger by altitude and distance. Here, tonight, I'm in a similar holding pattern. Circling above and beyond the danger. But like a plane that must eventually return to land when it runs low on fuel, I know that my disconnected elevation is temporary. The safety I perceive is an illusion.

As an Air Force pilot, I regained the earth between missions behind the fortified walls of whatever base I was at. At night, in my bunk, there was the vague notion of the enemy lurking out there in the ether beyond the base perimeter. And, occasionally, that enemy would lob a rocket or a mortar at us. Sometimes, someone would die. But there was always the feeling, or the illusion, of safety. Yes, I lived hyperaware, always with an eye toward the nearest hardened shelter or ditch where I could take cover if the air-raid sirens went off. But the idea of a base actually being overrun? Well, that's not a possibility I ever took seriously. We were always on the strong side of the fight.

Tonight, as I watch that distant battle, I slip into old habits from Iraq and Afghanistan, trying to recreate the illusion of safety I felt behind the fortifications at bases like Bagram and Balad. But those old habit patterns don't apply to this war. There are no fortifications here, and the enemy is at the gates. I'm no longer safely observing war from a cockpit, or tucked away inside a fortified perimeter. There are no US drones orbiting overhead to keep watch—only Russian drones choosing the next artillery target. No Phalanx Close-In weapons system to sound an air-raid alarm when a rocket is on its way. No, this is war by someone else's rules, and I'm smack in the middle of its destructive path. I realize I'm in danger, and I feel scared.

When I have enough to drink, I call my driver, a young man named Vasiliy, and tell him I'm ready to go. Minutes later he arrives. He has the radio turned off when I get in his little hatchback.

"Back to the hotel," I say.

"Okay."

We take off down the dark, sparsely lit streets. There's hardly another car on the road. No one is out walking tonight, and I spot only stray dogs as we zip along, descending back to town. With the radio off and in the darkness, I'm attuned to the hum of the wheels, the minute creaks of the suspension and the sound of Vasiliy pressing the pedals as he shifts gears.

"It seems tomorrow could be bad," Vasiliy says.

"Yes, it looks that way."

He pulls out a pack of cigarettes.

"You want one?"

"No thanks."

"Do you mind?"

"Not at all."

He rolls down his window a few inches and lights a cigarette.

"Do you have a way out?" he asks.

"No. Not really. I suppose I'll find a way west along the coast if things fall apart."

"Call me if you need. I'll drive you."

"I will."

"When it happens, it will happen quickly. You should be ready to go."

"I understand."

Back at the hotel I undress and get in bed. I feel comfortable and clean lying naked in the light coolness of the sheets. My head spins from the beers and with questions and imagined scenarios. I wonder if I'll look out the window in the morning and see tanks rolling down the street. If the separatists break through the Ukrainian lines, will they come this far? Will they clear out the hotel? How will they treat foreign journalists? Would it be safer to hole up in this hotel or try to flee west down the coast? If the city falls, how do I get back to Kyiv?

I think about James Foley for a moment. No way it could get that bad, I convince myself. But a chill goes down my spine, anyway.

As I wait for sleep to take me, I truly have no idea what tomorrow will bring. And I realize, despite all my persuasive bullshit, that I have no idea what to do.

* * *

Mariupol, Ukraine
September 5, 2014

The sounds of war began yesterday afternoon as a whisper.

After days of waiting for the Russian attack to begin on Mariupol, it was easy to believe the staccato, baritone thuds were imagined. But one by one people began to exchange awkward glances with one another, as if silently asking for confirmation of what they were hearing. Stray dogs and cats grew agitated. And after a few moments there was no mistaking the sound. It was real, the waiting was over. The battle had begun.

Today the concussions of artillery and rocket fire rattled windows in Mariupol. It seemed for a while that all was lost, and Russia's forces were poised to break through the Ukrainian lines and overrun the city. People were packing as much as they could into their cars and fleeing. Restaurants were shut down. The streets grew empty.

And then, as if ripped straight from the pages of *All Quiet on the Western Front*, the sounds of war went silent. In Minsk, Belarus—more than 700 miles north of Mariupol—Ukrainian and Russian politicians had reached a deal to stop the fighting. In an instant, armies of young men stopped shooting at each other.

The absurdity of war.

When the news hit Mariupol, it was like New Year's times a million. Passing drivers honked their horns. People cheered in celebration and strangers hugged each other.

Tonight I'm back in that same seaside bar from two nights ago. It's another beautiful night with an easy breeze. I'm drinking beer again, and the same awful techno covers of American songs are on the radio. It's as if the last few days are imagined.

But I can't stop thinking about what tonight could have been like.

It all started yesterday at 4 p.m. when Russia's forces launched from their stronghold 45 kilometers east of Mariupol in Novoazovsk. They attacked Ukrainian troops entrenched on the outskirts of Mariupol with heavy artillery, Grad rockets and tanks. The embattled Ukrainian units responded by deploying heavy artillery to the area and bombing enemy positions with fighter jets. Despite stiff resistance from the Ukrainian side, by lunchtime today it looked like the city was going to fall.

The streets emptied as people retreated indoors. The sounds of explosions and gunfire grew louder, and plumes of smoke from the fighting were visible from the seaside. The question on most everyone's mind was, "Should I stay or flee?"

I called my friend Nataly Oksanichenko to ask if she was okay. She and her husband, Leonid, have a young daughter named Veronica. For days they'd been debating what to do when the sack on Mariupol began.

"It's not so good right now," Nataly told me. "The sounds of explosions are getting louder, and it's scaring me."

The worry in her voice was clear.

Nataly decided to leave with Veronica for Leonid's grandparents' house west of the city, down the coast. Yet Leonid had to stay in Mariupol to close down his business, she explained. The young couple want to avoid becoming refugees and Leonid is doing what he can to shift his business from Mariupol to Kyiv before it's too late. But he thought he'd have more time before the fighting started.

"I was never patriotic before," Leonid said yesterday over lunch. "But if I wasn't married and didn't have a child I would be in some battalion. I am ready to defend my country, with my own life if I have to. I just don't see any other way for a good life for my family."

While her husband spoke, Nataly sat with her hands folded on the table. Her mannerisms and intonations were more subdued than

Leonid's. She'd resigned herself to the inevitability and hopelessness of the situation. She just wanted to leave.

"I'm scared because I have a little child," she said. "We have to leave. We don't have a future here."

Last night, with the Russian sack looking inevitable and imminent, Leonid made the impossible decision to send his wife and daughter away without him. He chose to stay, knowing what was probably about to happen here, rather than flee without a way to provide for his family.

"A year ago I would have thought you were crazy if you told me there was going to be a war here," Leonid told me. "Nobody wanted this."

The harsh realities of war.

Tonight Mariupol breathes a skeptical sigh of relief, but I think back to the feeling of a hurricane on the horizon and I wonder, "Has the storm passed, or is this only the eye of the storm? Is the worst still to come?"

I've been in war zones before. I'm familiar with the spectacle of combat and its associated emotions. But up until now the human experience of war for me has been limited to interacting with soldiers who have trained for combat and go into it willingly. Yesterday and today I experienced war in a completely new and alien way.

I saw the worry on the faces of a young couple as they decided to part ways amid the threat of invasion. I'll never forget that. It adds another layer to the absurd tragedy of war that I have never felt before.

To watch the streets empty, to see the fear on the faces of people passing by. To look into the eyes of a stranger and shake our heads in mutual disbelief as the sounds of an artillery barrage tear through the late summer breeze.

"Is this really happening?" our eyes say to each other.

It is, says the war.

Tank battles, heavy artillery, long-distance rocket attacks—this kind of combat is fucking terrifying.

But the terror is short-lived, and the cease-fire appears to be holding. The bars are open tonight in Mariupol. Across town young brides and grooms are getting married, following through on ceremonies put off for months by the war.

Life goes on.

Yet out there beyond the city streets, far away from the cheesy music and the embraces of newlyweds, the scars of the last two days of battle are still smoldering. After the fighting ended earlier today, I went out to see what this war really is.

Charred bodies dotted the freshly stilled battlefields. These were the bodies of men who did not die well. Not by the mercy of a gunshot to the head or the heart. Some had their bodies ripped apart by the concussion of artillery blasts. Some were missing limbs. Some lay with their insides spilled in the earth around them. Others burned to death, trapped inside the steel coffins their tanks became. Quite a few died in the way they had desperately clung to life—bodies halfway out of their ruined vehicles or splayed on the ground in fetal positions. Soldiers, frozen in the moment and the motion of their deaths like the plaster molds of the dead at Pompeii. Their lives ended today. The convenient forgetting about why they died begins tonight.

And still, as Mariupol celebrates, many more scared and tired soldiers wait in trenches and in tanks poised to once again release the dogs of war.

Walking Alone in a Foreign Country

I decided to leave Mariupol the day after the cease-fire. Despite my less than stellar Russian, I somehow successfully purchased a ticket at the train station and found my way to the right wagon and the "luxe" two-person sleeper berth that would be home for the 22-hour return journey to Kyiv.

In the train, I settled in and began to read.

The door opened and a tall man burst in the compartment. He was solidly built and sweating and two women helped carry his many bags.

"I hope I'm in the right seat," I said, probingly.

"Oh good, you speak English," one of the women said with a thick Russian accent. "My brother is from Canada."

"Nice to meet you," the tall man said in a huff and with a much lighter accent. "My name is Andrey." He was slightly breathless and had an out of sorts, disheveled air about him. He stuck out his hand.

"You too." I shook his hand. "My name is Nolan."

Andrey finished storing his bags in his half of the sleeper and gave me a nod and a half smile and left with one of the women. The other stayed for a moment longer.

"I feel better knowing my brother will have someone to talk to," she said, smiling, and then she spun out of the compartment. I went back to reading and put in my headphones. Some time later, right before the train left the station, Andrey came back in and plopped down on the bench defeatedly. Out of the corner of my eye as I read I could sense him making half glances at me, like he wanted to say something. As a writer I should have been more interested, but I was tired and empty after days in a war zone and I felt content to read and listen to my music and be completely within myself for a while.

Andrey moved over to the window and pressed up against the glass. Out on the platform were the two women who had brought him in the train. He alternated between waving and pressing his hand up against the glass as the train began to pull away. I saw his lips moving, silently mouthing words in a language I didn't know.

Soon the two women were out of sight and the train was on its way. Andrey plopped down again on the bench, his limbs loose with defeatism. Not out of despair, it seemed from my furtive glances, but from just being tired.

I took out my headphones.

"So you're from Canada?"

His chest was still moving quickly, but he seemed to be coming down from something.

"Yes, I'm Ukrainian but I lived in Canada for eight years and had a business there," he said. "And you?"

"I'm from Ameri... from the United States," I said, mindful of Canadian sensibilities about the word "American."

"What city are you from in Ukraine?" I asked.

"Donetsk."

I put down my book.

"How is it there?"

"Very, very bad," he said, folding one leg up onto the knee. He pushed both palms down into the bench. He spoke to me in side-glances. Now he was the one reluctant to talk.

"I fled to Mariupol with my wife, and we've been staying there with my sister. And then, well, everything started to go bad. I was going to leave last night but the fighting was too close. I thought I should leave today before it began again."

"What about your wife?" I asked.

"She's going back to Donetsk tomorrow," he said, becoming very sullen. He turned to look right at me. "She owns a business there and that's where our apartment and all of our things are. We want to move to Kyiv, but she's going back to get our winter clothes and some other things."

He exhaled and looked away.

"But I'm scared for her. It's a dangerous place."

"That's what I've heard."

"They stole my car you know," he said before telling me the story.

He was with his wife and another couple in Donetsk, driving somewhere, he couldn't remember where, when a gang of separatists pulled him over. They made the four of them get out and demanded he hand over his car.

"This is DNR property now," one of the separatists proudly proclaimed. "We need it for the revolution."

"It wasn't even a very nice car, it was just an old Audi," he told me. "But it didn't have tinted windows and had no bullet holes in it. It looked normal, which is what they wanted so they could get through the army checkpoints more easily."

Andrey thought about putting up a protest but decided it wasn't worth dying for a car. While all this was happening, a separatist commander, a woman, arrived with some others. She pressed Andrey to explain why he hadn't volunteered to join the separatist army.

"Are you an American spy?" she asked seriously.

He fumbled for an excuse, he explained to me. He knew if he said the wrong thing or if they discovered he had been living in Canada for eight years, they would either shoot him on the spot or take him to the separatists' headquarters in downtown Donetsk and torture him.

But before he could say anything, his wife spoke.

"He can't fight because I'm pregnant," she lied, patting her belly. "And I need him to take care of me."

"Ah, I understand," the woman said.

Andrey looked at me solemnly.

"You understand how dangerous it is in Donetsk?"

"I think so," I ventured. "I've also heard some bad stories about how they use civilians as human shields."

"Oh, let me tell you about that."

He explained how the separatists fired mortars and rockets from the tops of apartment buildings and schools and then fled, hoping to draw Ukrainian return fire that would kill civilians and make a good news clip for Russian propaganda. In one instance, he told me about an artillery attack, in which the separatists shot at buildings in Donetsk in a ruse to make it look like the Ukrainians were targeting civilians.

"You know what was funny," he told me. "The Russian TV crews were there a long time before the fire trucks or ambulances, a long time. But tell me, how would they know? How could they possibly get there so fast?"

He shrugged his shoulders, upturned his hands, and raised his eyebrows.

"You understand what I'm saying? They just do these things for the cameras."

He told me more. He told me about the checkpoints, and I said I knew about that. He said in Donetsk if you have a foreign passport or don't speak Russian, they consider you a spy. He was very adamant that I, as an American veteran, should not try to go to Donetsk.

"It would end badly for you," he said.

I agreed.

The constant artillery fire was terrifying. When it got really bad, shaking the ground like an earthquake, all Andrey and his wife could do was curl up on the floor and hope for the best. I asked why, if it was so dangerous there, did he and his wife stay for so long? I also asked why she had to go back.

"It's different in Ukraine than in the US," he said. "Most of us don't have mortgages or car loans. We own our apartments and cars outright and we save up our whole lives for them. They are all we have. If I leave my apartment and my other things, I can never get them back. I worked my whole life and now I'm 40 years old and I have nothing."

He told me his wife owned an outdoor sporting goods store in Donetsk, and she had to lock it up before they fled to Mariupol. They were just going to abandon the store and their home, he said.

She only had to make this one last trip and then she would meet him in Kyiv. He wanted go with her, but she convinced him it was too dangerous for a man to get back in and out through the checkpoints, especially hiding a Canadian passport. It was safer for a woman, she said. He knew his wife and her conviction and that he couldn't change her mind.

"This fucking war," he said disgustedly.

As the train moved north from Mariupol we watched on a map on my iPhone as we passed near the front lines of the battle that had raged the day before. Then, the train skirted within just a few dozen kilometers of Donetsk. As the kilometers between the war and us accumulated, the mood lightened. We talked about a lot of things. About life in America. Andrey told me about a road trip he took from Seattle to Chicago, and how amazed he was at the way different parts of America contrasted with each other.

He offered me some of the food he had with him, taking great pride in explaining to me how Ukrainians make cheese and the special spices used in preparing their version of jerky. And then he opened a bottle of cognac and he told me about his first wife and why that marriage had failed and how the woman to whom he was now married had changed everything for him.

"We get sad sometimes," he said, swirling the cognac in one of the ceramic mugs the train attendant had left us. "We ask, 'Why did we have to meet so late in life?'"

As the train went farther into the night, we went deeper into the bottle of cognac until it was gone. Andrey went to look for another.

"I should ask the stewardess if she has any," he said before he left, his words stumbling over the cognac. "Is that how you say it? Stewardess?"

"I think they prefer to be called to be flight attendants nowadays," I said, having had a good bit myself.

"From the flight attendant," Andrey proudly said to me as he returned a while later with another bottle.

I spread out on the bench on my side of the sleeper and rested my head up against the wall next to the window. He poured me another glass of cognac and left it on the small plastic table that was between us. I could reach the cup with my left hand without sitting up or looking for it.

"A good woman is a very, very rare thing," he said to me, speaking more slowly and with a thicker accent than before. "What do you think of Ukrainian women?"

"Very beautiful," I said.

"And my wife?"

"She's very Ukrainian."

"Yes, she certainly is," Andrey said as he sprawled out on his bench to stare at the ceiling. "I'm sorry, I think I'm getting a bit drunk."

We said a few more unimportant things before falling asleep.

The next morning I woke up to the high-pitched whistle of train brakes and the sun on my face through the window. Andrey was not in the cabin.

I got up and found the train attendant and asked for a coffee. After she brought it I sat by the window and watched the rolling fields of yellow sunflowers go by. After a while like this, the door slid open and Andrey came back. He was wearing a different shirt than the day before, a yellow one. He didn't say anything but sat down on the bench carefully and leaned forward with his elbows on his knees and with his cellphone in one hand. He talked without looking at me.

"They attacked Mariupol again last night."

"What, are you sure? What about the cease-fire? How do you know?"

"It started in the middle of the night. My wife called to tell me."

"So she didn't go to Donetsk then?"

A pause. He spun the cellphone in his hand.

"No. She still went. She said she had to."

It was my turn to talk but I didn't know what to say.

"This fucking war," he said for me.

A little while later we cleared the empty bottle of cognac from the small plastic table, threw away the cheese and jerky wrappers and returned the ceramic mugs.

For the rest of the train ride Andrey stood in the narrow hallway outside the door to our cabin, both hands grasped on the handrail that ran beneath the window out of which he silently stared.

After the train pulled into the Kyiv station, I helped him unload some of his bags and then we shook hands and exchanged phone numbers and emails. He said someone was coming to pick him up.

"Let's get a beer soon," I said.

"Yes, we should." His mind was somewhere else.

"Good luck, Andrey," I said. "I'll keep you and your wife in my thoughts."

"Thank you," he said, smiling with his lips only. His eyes were expressionless and gone.

I walked away and looked back one time before I turned the corner off the platform. Andrey was still standing where I had left him, talking on his cellphone as the crowd swirled around him.

*   *   *

Khreshchatyk, Kyiv's main boulevard, is closed to traffic on the weekends. The six-lane road becomes a pedestrian thoroughfare filled with artists, street performers, parents, children, and couples holding hands. A sharp change from what I had just seen on the war's front lines in Mariupol. And a long way from what happened on this street in February 2014, when under gray winter skies hundreds of thousands of protesters gathered during the revolution.

On the evening of my return from Mariupol in September 2014, the summer sky was clear and cool and people danced and sang and performed magic tricks where, months earlier, riot police had beaten protesters with batons and lobbed tear gas canisters, and where protesters burned tires as a smoke screen against the snipers who gunned down more than 100 people.

I put the sun at my back and walked into the crowd like I was the only one moving in that direction. A walk through a city of millions can be lonely if you don't speak the language. The foreign words in your ears form a blackout curtain between you and the people who swirl around you like fallen leaves. I remembered those lonely nights in Chicago, right after I had left the military, when I was so unsure about where to go next and what to do. As I've written before, coming back from war is a lot like walking alone in a foreign country. Memories of war end up living inside of you like memories of home. War, like being a foreigner, defines every atom of you. It's there with every step you take, making you hypersensitive to the world around you. Every street sign, every store front, every girl at whom you smile, every foot of pavement, every pigeon on the street or police officer at a street corner—you notice everything.

On the walk down Khreshchatyk, engrossed in my surroundings, I realized I hadn't thought about the war for a while; not until I saw a group of young soldiers walk past and I understood the war would always be there, even if I wasn't in it.

*　　*　　*

After Mariupol, I began to idle in Kyiv. I spent the nights in bars, drinking too much, yet churning out articles at a frenetic pace. Money was running low, however. At each trip to the ATM I watched my savings continue their slow erosion toward zero. My financial situation was like the doomsday clock, always just a few minutes to midnight.

"It's time to come home, Nolan," my mom told me in a phone call. "You've done enough."

I was annoyed and defiant. But I knew she was right.

My parents were, I believe, more anxious to get me away from the war than concerned by my finances. And I don't blame them. There was a sort of fatalism to my life in Ukraine, then. I'd nothing to come home to, and nothing to lose. I was isolated and losing perspective. I had left for Ukraine thinking I'd be gone for two, maybe three weeks. And now, three months later, I was scheming up ways to stay permanently, or at least until the war was over.

At night, alone, I would wander the streets with no destination in mind. Walking up and down Kyiv's many hills, along Khreshchatyk, down into Podil, then back up St. Andrew's and through the wide open squares in front of the illuminated domes of St. Michael's and St. Sofia's cathedrals.

I worried my life was equally as directionless as my late-night strolls. Surely, I thought, this all couldn't be just a random, one-off experience. No, this all had to mean something more.

Coming Home

Sarasota, Florida
October 2014

The war is still there, and so am I.

I'm in the checkout line at Trader Joe's in Sarasota. The conversation between the cashier and the guy in front of me goes something like this:

Cashier (holding a can of pumpkin puree): "Oh my God, this pumpkin is the best. Have you tried it?"

Man: "Of course! (Takes wallet out of his man-purse that he wears with its diagonal strap across his chest.) I love everything pumpkin in the fall. Have you tried the new pumpkin spice latte at Starbucks? Amazing."

Cashier: "Oh, I know. When you find something you like, you just have to gobble up as much as you can before it runs out."

In the checkout lane next to me, a middle-aged woman in Lululemon yoga pants holds a Louis Vuitton purse in the crook of her elbow with a BMW car key in that hand. In her other hand is an iPhone 6 in a pink protective case. She's talking to the cashier about a gluten-free diet.

I'm gone, watching everything from a perch 5,000 miles away in Ukraine, where I really am.

Am I back in reality, or have I left it?

The man in front of me says a few more things about pumpkin-flavored stuff and how much he likes fall and then he pays and walks away. I'm back. I step up to the cashier and put my bag of chicken breasts and wheat bread on the counter.

Cashier: "Well, how are you doing today, sweetie?"

How am I doing today? I don't know. I'm hardly here. I talk to the cashier in a sterile, out-of-body way. I pay and walk outside.

A shiny black Cadillac Escalade zips by, going too fast through the parking lot. Through the heavily tinted windows I see the driver look at me. I'm in Sloviansk, watching the buses take the soldiers to the front lines. There's one who looks right at me, and we make eye contact. He looks scared.

I get in my car and have to squeeze in because the one next to me has parked too close. I pull away and get on the road, and a young punk in a Japanese car with a spoiler tailgates me and then whips around and cuts me off. Suddenly I feel angry and I'm slipping back there but I pull myself from it. I put both hands on the steering wheel and breathe slow and hard and deep and think about the air going in and out of my lungs.

At a coffee shop earlier, I listened to some old men sitting around in high, leather-backed chairs. They sipped coffee and ate pastries and had polo shirts tucked into their Dockers shorts with one leg crossed over the other. They talked with authority about what America should do about ISIS and what Putin will do next. Traffic passed by out the window on the street behind them and the waiter came by and asked if they want anything else to eat or drink. Someone told a joke, I couldn't hear what it was, and they all laughed and started talking about something else.

It was like this coming home from Afghanistan and Iraq, I remember. Simple, ordinary things feel pointless and silly. It all feels familiar, and I know what comes next but am powerless to stop it.

Back home I sit on the couch and turn on the TV. There's a football game on. I see the young men in their uniforms and their old coaches. Then, I remember the Ukrainian soldiers in their mismatched uniforms with Kalashnikovs slung across their backs, holding the blue and yellow flag between them for a photo, smiling and giving me a peace sign. Looking back at the photo later I see one soldier in the corner with a stone-flat face looking away from the camera at something else. He's not scared, he's just not smiling. There's nothing in between. The tank battle came the next day. And the fighting is ongoing.

I think about fear. I think about the video of my friend James Foley and how he really didn't look all that scared right before he died. I wonder if I could be that strong, and then I'm back at that separatist checkpoint. I'm terrified and ashamed of my fear even though I'm not sure if I'm showing it.

Was it worth it to go? I had better not think about that, I tell myself. That is the one thing I should not think about.

But I do anyway.

I should have never left.

Then, I say to myself, "Yes, I had to."

But as a war correspondent you should never feel sorry about what war does to you. That's a trap. Life gave me every chance to avoid that war, and I went anyway. I know that but can't change how I feel.

I start to slip away again, but I stop myself. I'm good at that now. I want to get up from the couch but I can hardly sit up straight. After a while I just can't stand it any longer and I make some coffee for energy and leave for the gym.

Working out, I look in the mirror at my body. My veins and my muscles inflate and my arms look young and strong. And then it happens; it finally happens like a wave that has been cresting all day suddenly peaks and breaks apart.

Looking at the muscles of my arms in the mirror I'm back on the battlefields outside Mariupol hours after the cease-fire. There, on the ground, everywhere, lining the road, dead young bodies. Some, you can still see what they looked like when they were alive. Maybe a bullet or a piece of shrapnel killed the young man fast and easy. The others didn't die so well. Some with their insides spilled in the earth. I see them with their flesh and blood exposed and spread across the road and soaked into the green summer grass that rolls with the hills and blends with the blue sky in the distance. I look at the flesh beneath my skin in the mirror and I think of the charred flesh of the soldiers who had died trying to get out of their tanks that were burning and I, and I...

I look over and the young kid on the workout bench is looking at me funny. I'm sweating and realize I've been staring at the mirror for a while, I don't know for how long.

I finish working out and the effort takes me back to now, clears my head and makes me feel calm. I leave the gym and drive out to Ringling Bridge, which crosses Sarasota Bay to Bird Key. I park my car and start walking across the bridge with the long rays of the setting sun over the Gulf of Mexico in front of me. A couple walk by holding hands.

I'm back on Khreshchatyk the night after I returned to Kyiv from Mariupol. In the crowd, I'm the only one moving at this speed as the sun sets behind me. I walk the bridge, but I'm not here. I'm back there. I look through everyone I pass. I keep walking. I remember the nights I wandered Kyiv alone, trying to think of ways to write about a forgotten war.

That's it, I think, I just have to write about it. That's what I'll do.

I go home and shower and change. I take my laptop to a café downtown. I open it on the table and start a new word document. I try to write, but I feel empty and when I try to let it flow nothing comes. I order a beer and the alcohol calms me and everything doesn't feel like it's moving so fast anymore. I start to write. Probably not well, but at least I'm writing. After a while it's all used up and I feel better. But I know that alcohol is a crutch and I tell myself that I won't lean on it any more. I think about the train rides to the front lines and how I wanted to write but I couldn't, about how I wanted to eat but wasn't hungry. I think about the train ride out of Mariupol the morning the cease-fire fell apart. I was shaking off my hangover from the cognac the night before. And there's my friend, Andrey, staring out the window, worrying about his wife stuck behind the lines in Donetsk.

"This fucking war," he says, knowing he's going the wrong direction as the train glides through fields of yellow sunflowers.

I feel the same way here, in Sarasota. Someone with a cup of gelato in hand walks by, and someone else passes by with a dachshund on a leash. There are some older people sitting outside at a plastic table with glasses of white wine in between them. I'm here, surrounded by this, but I'm not present. I'm passing by on my way somewhere else. I feel the same dread like I'm on that train from Kyiv again, heading to Mariupol and the war in the middle of the night. Or maybe it's more like I'm Andrey, stuck on a train going in the wrong direction. Feeling like the war is where I should be.

I open Facebook and check the feeds of my friends back in Ukraine. They say the fighting is back on and getting worse. I read the news. There's talk now of separatist violence in Ukraine's second biggest city, Kharkiv. And Dnipropetrovsk, a city of more than one million people, is bracing for an attack.

"We're digging trenches and laying mines," the deputy governor of Dnipropetrovsk says. "If the Russians try to invade this city, it will be their Stalingrad."

I was here for minute, but I'm gone again. Taken away, back to where I never left. And then I know I'll never leave, and it becomes so obvious that I'll never be totally back.

I finish my beer and order another.

I read once that no one you love is ever truly lost. That's true, and so is this—no war is ever truly over. Even if it isn't your own.

The Way Back

During the winter of 2014, as the war in Ukraine simmered under its first cease-fire, I returned to Florida and basically picked up where I'd left off, as if Ukraine had never even happened. But Ukraine had become the ever-present center of gravity to each and every thought. Desperately, I searched for a way back.

After some weeks living with my parents in Sarasota, I decided to move to Washington, DC. I had nothing waiting for me there, only the faint hope of finding a job that could finance my way back to Ukraine. So, I did what I'd learned to do best—I loaded whatever was left of my whittled-down personal effects into my Jeep and put the rest in a storage unit. Then I said my goodbyes and without any fanfare or much ado slipped out of town and drove north.

I stopped for a night at Sea Island, Georgia, and splurged for a room at the Cloister, a beautiful resort hotel dating back to the 1920s. In the evening I was alone, ordering Old Fashioneds and thinking about Ukraine, when the barman snapped me out of my introspective tailspin and we got to talking. He shook his head in disbelief as I described the battle for Mariupol. I recounted how the rumble and flashes of the artillery at night were like a Florida thunderstorm. I explained the dilemmas faced by young families, like my friends Leonid and Nataly Oksanichenko.

The barman wiped clean a beer glass and shook his head. "You never see anything about all that in the news," he said. "It's a shame, really."

He gave me another drink on the house.

"What you do takes a lot of guts, man," he said. "It's damn heroic, if you ask me."

I said thanks and enjoyed the Old Fashioned, but I felt awkward at the compliment. Whenever someone thanked me for my service in the military, I always felt a little silly about it, too. But truly, such accolades were precious. It was like that for most people in the military, I suspected. It didn't matter if it was lip service praise, or truly sincere. It meant we weren't forgotten. That was enough.

As a war correspondent, however, words like brave, hero, or courage—well, they all seemed misplaced. Such words belonged to someone else. Yes, there is a degree of guts required to walk head-on into a war zone. Moving toward the sounds of gunfire and artillery is about as scary as scary can be. But that's not heroism. Heroism, at least to me, implies a degree of selflessness. By that measure, my reasons for going to war as a journalist were far too selfish for me to be called a hero. Real heroes don't search for reasons to be heroic.

*   *   *

My days in Washington that winter were initially fruitless. I wrote to every news outlet I knew of, trying to explain why they should hire me to go back to Ukraine. I said there was a real war going on, that the cease-fire was a farce, and that the war could very easily spiral into something much worse. To paraphrase the response I typically received: "Thank you, but no one cares about Ukraine."

There were some hard times, then. Again, like that summer in Key West, I wondered what had become of my life. How had I become a rootless nomad, living out of my car one day, and in a spare room in some basement apartment I'd found on Craig's List the next? To be frank, war reporting was an out. If I landed a gig, even as a freelancer, I could skip the country and live out of a backpack for a few years. I didn't need much.

I lucked into a job in Washington at Northwestern University's National Security Journalism program. I was grateful for the income and the résumé bullet. But, at that time, with the war in Ukraine heating up again, it was a bit soul-crushing to work in an office. I kept looking for a way back.

That February, as I sat in my apartment about to meet some friends for a beer, I received an email from my friend Valentyn Onyshchenko. He wrote that he was trapped in a basement in the eastern Ukrainian town of Debaltseve, which was at that moment under a heavy artillery bombardment. He thought he was going to die.

"We're fucked man," Valentyn wrote. "I'm in Debaltseve, the separatists surrounded us, I don't know if I will make it outta here, just wanted to tell that it was very nice knowing you, I can't hear now because of the explosions near me, take care man, and god bless America and Ukraine!"

For weeks, Russian regular forces used artillery, mortar, and rocket bombardments to pummel the Ukrainian troops in and around Debaltseve. The only refuge from the onslaught was to seek shelter underground. That's what many Ukrainian soldiers and civilians did. And that's how many of them died. The United Nations later reported that the bodies of more than 500 Ukrainian civilians had been found in houses and in cellars throughout the town. Some were entombed when their homes collapsed onto them due to a direct hit. Others suffocated when incendiary devices sucked the oxygen out of the air.

Valentyn's email left me hollowed out and unable to move. I just sat there, rereading his words again and again. I heard the sound of people outside my apartment on the sidewalk, laughing, talking, totally oblivious to the life-and-death drama my friend was enduring so far away. I canceled on my friends and fired off another barrage of emails, pitching my proposal to report on the war to news sites around the world.

Finally I caught the break I'd been looking for.

The Heritage Foundation's news site, The Daily Signal, hired me to cover the war in Ukraine as a full-time foreign correspondent. They offered to pay me a monthly salary and cover expenses, including my body armor. Plus, and most valuably, I had the editorial freedom to cover the war according to my own moral compass. It was the dream job. Now, it was time to do what I had done so many times before—disappear. But it isn't easy to live shallow, no matter how temporary you might consider a place to be. Inevitably, your life leaves a footprint.

That winter I'd been dating a woman named Jenny, and things had been going fast. We were already talking about love and the future. She was about to move from Washington to San Francisco, and I thought about going with her. So, when I got the offer from The Daily Signal that February to go back to Ukraine, I pretended like I would only be away for a few months. But the truth is, I was already gone for good. I canceled my lease, quit my job at Northwestern, and drove back home to Florida to see my parents. Jenny came down to visit for a few days. It was the last time I ever saw her.

Valentyn survived the Debaltseve battle. We've had more than a few beers in the intervening years to celebrate his brush with death.

Good and Evil

Kyiv, Ukraine
May 2015

Mikael Skillt sits before me in a plywood hut at the Azov Battalion's barracks in an abandoned industrial park on the outskirts of Kyiv. Outside, there's the sound of hammering as civilian volunteers and troops build a classroom and finish a CrossFit workout area. They're constructing from scratch a military training facility for the volunteer paramilitary unit's more than 1,400 soldiers.

Periodically, a soldier will open the door to the small room. Seeing the Swedish sniper inside, he lowers his head deferentially and apologizes for interrupting.

"The myth is more exciting than reality," Skillt says with a sheepish smile. "But when you're in heavy fire, it feels like all the guns in the world are pointed at your position. So when I, as a sniper, can make the firing stop for a guy, it makes me their hero."

With close-cropped reddish-blond hair and a beard, Skillt's easy-going demeanor matches his matter-of-fact way of speaking. He's quick to make a self-deprecating joke, but rarely breaks eye contact while talking.

On this day in May 2015, the then–38-year-old Swede wears US multicam fatigues with a Ukrainian army sniper badge pinned to his left breast. He looks a little softer now than in some of the pictures of him on the front lines a year earlier, the result of the more sedentary life he leads as an instructor at the Azov Battalion's Kyiv base—and, he adds, due to his Ukrainian girlfriend's cooking.

"Ukrainian women don't like skinny men," he says with a grin.

A year and a half earlier, Skillt's current life would have been unthinkable. Before the war, he was in and out of jail in Sweden and pretty much adrift in life. A military veteran who served as a sniper in the Swedish National Home Guard, Skillt had also been a member of Sweden's far right and a spokesman for several neo-Nazi groups.

"I was the representative of evil," he says.

* * *

Cowards. That's what Skillt thought as he pored over photos and YouTube videos of the carnage playing out on Kyiv's central square, the Maidan, in February of 2014.

The snipers bothered him most. Why didn't they just shoot the protesters in the leg? And why shoot protesters at all, anyway? What threat did a man in a bicycle helmet and a metal shield really pose to police in riot gear? People were dying. And there he was, working a construction job in Stockholm. Out of the action. Useless.

"Something woke up in me," Skillt explains. "Maybe it was the warrior mentality."

Ready to join the revolution, the Swede bought a one-way ticket to Kyiv for February 28, 2014. He told his boss he'd be gone for a few days and explained to his girlfriend why he had to go to Ukraine.

"Our relationship went from not the best in the world to the worst," Skillt says, chuckling. "And that was the end of it."

Former Ukrainian President Viktor Yanukovych fled on February 21, and four days later the revolution was over. When Skillt arrived in Kyiv, he had "missed the whole shebang."

But that March Russia invaded Crimea and a Kremlin-orchestrated separatist movement took hold in Ukraine's eastern Donbas region. There was talk of war and protest groups born on the Maidan, like the Azov Battalion, began to morph into paramilitary units. Skillt had found his ticket to war.

"We could see something bad was going to happen," he says. "The only reason we didn't go to Crimea is because we had no guns."

As a sniper in the Swedish National Home Guard, Skillt had never seen combat. Experiencing war remained an elemental part of his being that he'd not yet satisfied. Thus, the war in Ukraine offered a path to self-actualization.

"Ukraine gave me purpose," Skillt says, "and I think a man needs a purpose."

When Skillt joined the Azov Battalion in the spring of 2014, it was still a civilian volunteer partisan group operating outside the bounds of governmental oversight. Whether due to battlefield compromises necessary for victory or a genuine change of heart, Skillt worked with governments around the world—including Israel, the U.S., and his native Sweden—to build the Azov Battalion from a civilian volunteer battalion with about 100 soldiers into a Ukrainian National Guard battalion sanctioned by the Ministry of Internal Affairs, with personnel topping 1,400 and bases throughout Ukraine. Despite the unit's growth, in the summer of 2015 many of its soldiers only receive two weeks of formal instruction before deploying to the front lines.

The Azov Battalion played a key role in the early months of the Ukraine war, most notably in the defense of Mariupol. Yet, the unit was excluded from the US military's training mission in western Ukraine due to its alleged neo-Nazi ideology.

It's true that a minority of soldiers with far-right, neo-Nazi persuasions exist within the Azov Battalion's ranks. And those soldiers do little to hide their beliefs. Some have tattoos of the Nazi swastika on their bodies. Others wear jewelry with Nazi symbols and read Adolf Hitler's book, "Mein Kampf," at night in their bunks. But most of the Azov Battalion soldiers I meet say they're fighting for Ukraine's sovereignty and to repel what they call a "Russian invasion" of their homeland. Those with far-right convictions live and fight side-by-side soldiers from 22 countries and various backgrounds, including Arabs, Russians, and Americans—as well as Christians, Muslims, and Jews.

"In any army there is always a little bit of bad meat," Skillt offers. "For example, when I was in the Swedish army, I was that little percentage of bad meat. But is a man's desire to die for his country or a cause any less heroic if he is a nationalist?"

For his part, Skillt doesn't shy away from discussing his neo-Nazi past. In fact, he talks about it openly, referring to his earlier beliefs as "misguided" and "idiotic." He also claims his service in the Ukraine war shattered his previously held stereotypes and spurred him to abandon National Socialism.

"I'm not a Nazi, and I don't believe in National Socialism," he tells me. "When I got to Ukraine 17 months ago, I was a real bastard. I had stereotypes against Jews, blacks, Arabs. But I've fought with them, and now they are like brothers. Before, some things were black and white. But now I know nothing is certain. Good and bad people come in all colors. The world is very gray."

In Ukraine, Skillt is largely seen as a hero. Yet, Skillt's self-proclaimed ideological evolution has also left him a pariah among neo-Nazi groups in his homeland. Sweden's far-right movement, which largely celebrates Russian President Vladimir Putin for his conservatism and hard line against homosexuality and immigration, frequently accuses Skillt of being on the wrong side of the war.

"Russia calls me a Nazi bastard, and my old friends in Sweden call me a Jew-lackey," Skillt says. "I'm having an identity crisis."

* * *

Later on, Skillt and I walk together to the Azov Battalion's base in the center of Kyiv. It's a nondescript building just a block away from the Maidan. Inside, there are portraits of fallen soldiers on the walls, as well as posters emblazoned with the unit's controversial symbol. Soldiers say the Azov Battalion's symbol stands for "Idiya Natsii," in Ukrainian—or, "Idea of the Nation." Others, however—including many foreign journalists—say the symbol is way too close to the Nazi Wolfsangel to be a coincidence.

In a unit that eschews traditional military rank and protocol, combat experience is the ultimate measure of a man and the respect he's due within the Azov Battalion. Still, there's a sense of strict discipline among the soldiers, especially the younger ones who show great humility before the combat-tested veterans. Accordingly, the Azov Battalion's troops treat Skillt like a superior officer. They stand when he enters a room and pull to the side of a hallway when he passes. Nearly everyone offers Skillt the Azov Battalion's unique handshake—hands clasped around forearms like a medieval warrior or a viking would do.

The new recruits are evidently nervous about what they will face in battle. You can easily see that fear in their eyes as they mill about the hallways. Consequently, the combat veterans in their midst possess a mystical aura because they have already answered the most basic and burning question for any soldier on the eve of battle—*Am I brave?*

You never know, really, how you'll be when the time comes. Will some inner hero emerge, as you hope? Or, are you truly a coward? There's no way to know unless you go to war. It's like high-altitude mountaineering. Some people, like the Sherpas I met in Nepal, are genetically gifted to adapt to the thin air and limited oxygen at high altitude. Either you're born with the gift or you're not. Your talent has nothing to do with physical fitness or training. In that sense, war and mountains are the truest tests of a person's inner nature. You can't improve your genetic ability to acclimatize to high altitude, and you can't fake courage under fire. The only way to know if you can survive a mountain is to climb it. It's the same way with war and courage.

Within the Azov Battalion's ranks, the combat veterans maintain a paternal air around the green, untested soldiers. It's a simple relationship. The new soldiers depend on the combat veterans for their survival. And the combat veterans retain a protective instinct to keep the rookies alive. There's no institutional bedrock to the Azov Battalion like there is in the US military. Collectively, there are no traditions to uphold, and most troops have no desire to advance in rank or pursue careers as professional soldiers. This is a military unit forged specifically for the war it's fighting. Consequently, bureaucratic busywork is virtually nonexistent, as is any notion of careerism. The Azov Battalion's soldiers have a war to fight and win. Nothing else matters. It is, in the truest sense, a warrior tribe.

In the hallway, Skillt meets a towering soldier who goes by the nom de guerre "Spider." Spider has warm, sensitive eyes, and a friendly enough demeanor. But on his hand I notice a small black tattoo—the letters, "SS." Discreet evidence of something sinister. Skillt introduces me. Spider smiles and shakes my hand and offers to meet us out for a beer. We agree. I have my reservations, but I want to understand.

An hour or so later, Skillt and I meet Spider and some other Azov Battalion soldiers at a downtown pub. One young soldier has a tattoo across the back of his shaved head; it reads, "100 percent racist." Another soldier wears a necklace with a swastika pendant.

The troops won't let me pay for anything. They ask me many questions about the wars in Iraq and Afghanistan. And then they tell me stories—intimate tales about friends who died in combat. There's little posturing, the soldiers freely admit to the fear they feel in combat. When I ask what they're fighting for, they all say roughly the same thing: to defend their country from a Russian invasion. I can't help but admire these men for their courage and patriotic convictions. But I also feel uneasy, on edge, as if I'm in the midst of some dark and dangerous force. Like I'm passing my finger through a candle flame... I keep moving so I don't get burned.

Still, I want to be friendly with these men. I remember meeting that Taliban fighter in Srinagar and wonder if it's more natural to want to combat or befriend an enemy. In what direction does the momentum of humanity more naturally flow—toward peace or toward war? In any case, I feel a desire to understand these men, even if I find their ideology abhorrent.

After a few rounds of beers the troops ask if I want to join them at another bar. I agree. When we arrive there a little later, the place is nearly empty. This band of about a dozen Azov Battalion soldiers rolls in and practically owns the place. They're all dressed in black T-shirts and jeans. Their Nazi tattoos are clearly visible, but no one seems to care. The bouncer is a friend of the soldiers, and he turns a blind eye to the weapons they carry. Some have pistols tucked into the back waistband of their jeans. Some have knives—big Rambo-worthy blades.

I keep thinking, "Is this real life?"

We order drinks, and the toasts begin. The troops call me a friend of Ukraine, a patriot. Then they chant: "Glory To Ukraine! Glory to heroes! Death to our enemies!"

Sometime near dawn, Skillt and I step out for cigarettes. Outside, in the sobering chill and quiet of the waning night, we talk seriously about the war. I ask Skillt about his first time in combat.

It was in Mariupol, he tells me, in the opening months of the war in June of 2014. He'd been in plenty of fights before then, Skillt explains, but true combat remained a mystery to him at that time. Above all, he wondered whether he'd be brave. Skillt says he found the answer to that question at a road crossing when the enemy shot at him with a 50-caliber machine gun.

"The enemy drew first blood," he recalls. "I froze, and I thought, 'This is how it's going to end.'"

At first, Skillt says he was paralyzed. Not by fear, but by over-whelming sensory overload. He quickly snapped out of it, he explains, experiencing for the first time what he later refers to as "work mode." Thoughts, emotions, and sensations that weren't necessary to his survival fell away; the universe reduced to the singularity of the here and now.

"All the things that kind of make Mikael, Mikael—those things go away," Skillt tells me. "The speaking, the laughing. Normally I can't run for six hours, but when I go into 'work mode,' I can. I can jump higher. I react much quicker. I don't speak very much at all. Everything just zooms out. I don't know what's happening. You peel off what's human to become some sort of robot."

Sunrise is close at hand; the night is nearly over. Before we go back inside, I ask Skillt one last question: "What did it feel like to kill for the first time?"

"I actually thought it would feel really, really bad," Skillt replies. "But in the end, I didn't feel much. I wish I never had to kill a man, because once you do it, you cross a big moral line. But I know if I don't do it, this guy might kill my friends."

He pauses for a pull on his cigarette. Then he adds, "You never know how it's going to be. You really don't know."

* * *

There is a moral cost to war that reveals itself in the way a soldier lives in peace. In many ways, life in peace is more complicated. The black-and-white, kill-or-be-killed simplicity of battlefield morality doesn't exist. In war, a soldier is temporarily relieved of the moral consequences of his or her actions by the necessity of duty. When duty is a memory, however, soldiers can question the things they've done. The line blurs between right and wrong. "Work mode," that protective cloak that shuts off the emotional hesitation to do what is necessary, no longer exists.

For me, the overall justice of the war in Ukraine is black and white. But there's a moral gray zone when considering the character of soldiers like Mikael Skillt. Yes, his cause was just, but Skillt was a complicated man who lived in the no man's land between good and evil. In the past, he believed repugnant things. There's no doubt about that. But he renounced his sins and fought courageously in defense of a just cause. There's no doubt about that, either.

Still, I can't turn a blind eye to what those swastikas represent. I can't ditch my belief in the categorical imperative and the conclusion that, yes, it does matter what lies in the wellspring of a soldier's heart.

Over dinner in Kyiv, I ask Skillt whether war had ultimately proven to be a path to redemption, or ruin, for his soul. The Swedish sniper leans back, takes a long sip of beer, and considers my question. It's been a few weeks since that night out at the bars. On this evening, we're sitting in an outdoor, tented terrace at a restaurant in the city center. It's raining sheets and a soccer match is on the television.

"War can bring a man to destruction or help him to reach new heights," Skillt says at last, looking into the rain. "War peels off every

Above: On the flight deck of the USS George H. W. Bush *in May 2017. Each day about 16 to 24 sorties launched from the carrier en route to Iraq and Syria to support the coalition air war against ISIS.*

Left: Waiting for the all-clear signal after a Taliban rocket attack at Forward Operating Base Shank in Afghanistan in December 2013.

With my brother, Drew in Afghanistan in 2013. Seeing him in the war zone suddenly made me very aware of the dangers I faced.

On the front lines in the embattled town of Shyrokyne in eastern Ukraine in April 2015. Trenches, tank battles, artillery barrages—it was a terrifying type of warfare that I'd never experienced before.

The unmerciful end of the world. Marking the Himalayan border between India and China at an altitude of 13,500 feet, Pangong-Tso is the highest salt-water lake in the world.

Ukrainian soldier Konstantin Bernatovich on patrol in the embattled Ukrainian town of Pisky in June 2015. The constant drumbeat of artillery highlighted the fact that, despite multiple cease-fires, the war had never ended.

Konstantin and Marina Kasyanenko present the uniform of their son Daniel, a 19-year-old Ukrainian soldier who died in battle. "He went to war as a boy and came back as a wise old man," Marina told me.

A typical scene in the front-line town of Pisky in eastern Ukraine. It's amazing how normal things stand out as being so extraordinary when you're in a war zone.

Tsering Tunduk at his home on Pangong-Tso lake. In 1969 the refugee joined an all-Tibetan unit in the Indian army to avenge his parents' death at the hands of Chinese soldiers.

The artist Pemba Nuru at his home in the Himalayas. Nuru lost all his fingers and toes to frostbite while crossing the Himalayas to escape Communist rule in Tibet.

On the way to the Nangpa La, the Himalayan pass used by thousands of Tibetans to escape China into Nepal. I didn't see another human on the weeklong trek to the top of the pass on the Nepal–China border.

The simple way of life in Nepal's Himalayan region was a reprieve from the hustle and bustle of modern life.

After years of constant combat, the war in Ukraine became a long-distance artillery standoff. At some places, no man's land between Ukrainian and Russian forces was several kilometers across. At others, the two camps were close enough to shout insults at each other.

Kurdish peshmerga soldiers on patrol in Sinjar, Iraq, the site of a notorious ISIS genocide. The Kurds had already discovered about 100 mass graves by the time I arrived in May 2016.

Above: A U.S. soldier in Afghanistan in December 2013. America's volunteer fighting force represents less than 1 percent of the total population. Consequently, the trauma and sacrifice of combat is shouldered by only a small, select slice of the country.

Left: My mom made a surprise trip to the U.S. Air Force Academy to visit me following basic training in the summer of 2000. Here, we share a quiet moment.

On patrol with Ukrainian soldiers in June 2015. A walk through Pisky was a testament to how destructive artillery can be.

On the summit of 20,305-foot-tall Island Peak in Nepal in October 2011 beside my guide, P. K. Sherpa, on the left. The climb was a true challenge, but, in the end, it didn't change anything.

An unforgettable dinner at a peshmerga fort in Iraq in May 2016. Outside, we could hear the sounds of U.S. airstrikes on ISIS forces. "Before, we had no friends but the mountains," General Omar Hama Ali Farag, right, told me. "Now we have America, too."

Sunrise in Afghanistan the day after a Taliban rocket almost killed me. War, above all, teaches you how much you want to live and how little that matters.

My father and I at Tampa airport the morning of my first departure for Ukraine in the summer of 2014. "I'm so tired of sending my sons off to war," my dad said with tears in his eyes as he hugged me goodbye.

layer of your humanity. But, in the end, war made me into a much better person.''

Daniel

There were a lot of ways to die in Pisky. Snipers, artillery, mortars, booby-traps, gun battles. That was the worst part of this war. You just never knew when it was going to happen.

And yet, you went on living out of habit. You got used to the explosions and the gunfire—it's amazing, really, what we humans can get used to. You let down your guard. You stood outside for some sun and to drink your morning coffee. In sandals and a tank top you walked the hundred yards from the cellar, in which you hid from the artillery, to the outhouse and the toilet. During the day you would walk through the ruined town on patrol, spending hours outside to get an interview or some photos. But in your mind you were always ready for it to start. And you were always worried that you might get it.

The artillery threat was practically unending, with only the occasional lull. You got used to it, and when it wasn't all that close you hardly paid attention. You only took cover when there was a certain treble in the way the explosions cracked, meaning it was nearby.

You were in no rush to get out of bed in the morning. You enjoyed being in bed in the cool cellar with the warm blankets as you pretended the booms and the gentle vibrations were from a summer thunderstorm and not the war.

There was a loud, high-gain crack, which flowed into a longer, ground-shaking boom. You went outside and saw a burning crater where the shell had landed in the courtyard just 30 feet from the entrance to the cellar. And then you had breakfast. You waited a while before walking out the courtyard, across the street to the outhouse and the shower. Sitting in the outhouse, the daylight came in at the random angles of the different shrapnel holes in the wall and door. While pouring a bucket of cold water on yourself in the shower shed, you laughed, thinking how funny it would be if the shelling started right then and you had to run back to the cellar naked and covered in soap suds.

In Pisky, the Minsk II cease-fire was a farce. Russian artillery pummeled Ukrainian positions daily, and the Ukrainian soldiers responded in kind. But it wasn't just the daily artillery exchanges that illuminated the absolute absurdity of pretending this war was at a truce. The Ukrainian soldiers in Pisky joked that they were guinea pigs for all of Russia's new weapons. They had, of course, been hit by the regular stuff: 152 mm SAU mobile artillery units, 120 mm artillery, 80 mm mortars, grenades, and machine guns. But they also got it from tanks, and Grad and Smirch rockets. Most said the Russians' automatic grenade launcher was what they feared the most.

"You will look like hamburger if you are caught in the open when they shoot with the grenades," a sniper named Volodymyr told me.

The nastiest weapons were the white phosphorus shells. There was an impact hole made by one about three feet away from the outhouse we all used. No crater, just a perfectly circular entry hole that went more than ten feet down into the black soil. White phosphorus rounds were designed to bore down into basements and set fires—a way to kill soldiers as they slept and ate. There was no safe place in Pisky. The fear of death was a constant companion.

* * *

Train travel is an ordinary experience. In Ukraine, I went to war that way.

During the six-hour trip to the eastern war zone I listened to Jack Johnson on my iPhone and munched on an Egg McMuffin that I'd picked up from the McDonald's at the Kyiv train station. I was on my way to embed with the Ukrainian regular army's 93rd Mechanized Brigade in the front-line town of Pisky, just about a mile outside the embattled Donetsk Airport and where some of the war's most intense combat had taken place.

A walk through Pisky was a testament to how destructive artillery can be. The landscape was lifeless, abandoned, militarized. A cratered moonscape in places. Shrapnel holes pockmarked virtually every vertical surface in town. Even courtyard doors of quarter-inch-thick steel looked like Swiss cheese. Most buildings had a section of roof caved in from a direct hit and windows were invariably shattered. Even the weather was tainted. A sunny day or a starry night were no longer things to enjoy but portended danger from the Russian drones constantly buzzing overhead.

This was a long-distance war in which the two sides hardly ever saw each other except through binoculars or a drone feed. Artillery was lobbed back and forth every day. Sometimes the tanks would come out, too, maneuvering to different positions to fire off a few rounds before returning to their hiding places. The sound of tank treads clanking was never good.

Two soldiers had picked me up from the small town of Kostiantynivka, where the rail lines ended before the eastern front, to drive me the rest of the way to Pisky. On the way in, I was impressed by the myriad vignettes of normal life out the window. A shirtless boy on a bicycle, a mother cradling an infant, an old woman on a cell phone. All evidence of life somehow carrying on despite the war. It's amazing how normal things stand out as being so extraordinary when one is traveling into a war zone. The most important part of any war story is neither the clash of armies nor the perversion of politics—it's the tragedy of life interrupted.

A couple miles from the front lines, the artillery rumble became noticeable from inside the moving vehicle. We drove over a bridge that crossed a lake. Off to the side I saw a group of children swimming, taking turns diving off a floating platform. Then, one hundred meters after the bridge, we stopped at the last army checkpoint before the war zone. The pickup snaked through the concrete and steel tank barricades and barbed wire. The soldier standing at the block post waved us through. And that was it, the threshold from peace to war. The war in Ukraine was a destination. Once you're at it, you're in it.

The artillery was a blind, impersonal threat. Consequently, surviving artillery was all about the odds. About not being in the wrong place at the wrong time. The artillery was a constant worry, but the snipers inspired a different kind of fear. A soldier fires an artillery shell at a coordinate, not with a human in the crosshairs like a sniper does. When a sniper shoots at you it's personal. All you can do is run and hope and listen to the whistle of passing bullets. A sniper's bullet wasn't a haphazard shot fired into the ether of war like a mortar or a rocket. It was an intimate act committed by another human who wanted to kill you.

Once, as I was walking through Pisky, the wall beside me erupted in a geyser of plaster and paint just a few feet ahead. I never heard the shot. A dazed instant passed as I processed what had happened. Sniper. Then I ran for my life. The effort of running at a full sprint while wearing body armor was overwritten by adrenaline and focus. My whole world condensed to the spot up the street where I could turn into the safety of a walled-in courtyard and the entrance to the basement where the Ukrainian soldiers and I lived. I ran as fast as my legs would go and burst into the basement, breathing heavily and clearly rattled. Inside, some soldiers sat at the table having breakfast. One was lying on a couch reading a book. Everyone looked up at me like a record had just skipped to a stop. I dropped my helmet and leaned over with my hands on my knees.

"*Kak dela?*" a soldier named Bogdan asked. How are you?

"Sniper," I replied through my heaving breaths. No translation needed.

They laughed, and all I could do was laugh about it, too.

*　　*　　*

The louder the artillery, the louder the laughter and joking at the dinner table. As if jokes and laughs comprised a force field from the dangers outside. We were, in fact, relatively safe from shrapnel in the cellar. But a direct hit would be catastrophic. But what can one do? Only wait and distance the mind from the danger by the collective defense of camaraderie. When the shelling grows louder, you feel a need to be around others. If you're sleeping in your bunk, perhaps reading or listening to music, and the walls start to shake from artillery, it's an automatic reaction to get up and walk to the kitchen table where the others are gathered. You sit down, they pour you a drink, you clink glasses. They nod and smile at you, slap you on the back, and then it's all okay. Your fear clears like an early morning mist in the sun. A warm, calming shiver flows through you from head to toe better than a shot of hard alcohol.

We were sitting around the table like that one night after dinner when a 19-year-old soldier named Daniel Kasyanenko came by for a visit. It was dark when he arrived, hours past when he was supposed to have left his post. He had been in a battle that evening, he said, a bad one. There was sniper and machine-gun fire, and artillery falling all around. He wasn't even able to shoot back, he said, because it was so intense. He could only low-crawl through the trenches to find cover and wait it out. Yet, when describing the battle, he said: "It was really awesome. Really awesome." He gave a thumbs-up and smiled broadly.

He looked tired, though. The young man immediately chugged several glasses of water and then juice as soon as he sat down. Vasiliy, one of the older soldiers, filled Daniel's plate with food. The young man ate well and glided easily into the conversation, as if he were getting home from afternoon sports practice rather than a day of combat.

Daniel had a soft, tanned face, small dark eyes, and patchy young man's beard, which he had let grow around his neckline and upper lip like many other young Ukrainian soldiers. He wore a cross on his wrist, I noticed. His manner of speech was staccato, halting, and he sometimes stared off when stuck on a word, either due to the translation or because he was explaining an idea that is hard to express in any language. Daniel was unique in his ability to put the toll of the war in context. Although only 19, he understood the inalterable changes occurring in him. He recognized that he was spending the formative years of his manhood in a place where all that life owed him—years, love, family, career—could disappear any second in a white flash and red heat and dark nothing. Only the fate of seconds and inches decided what life truly owed you in Pisky. You were either one of the lucky ones, or a name that they made a toast to before dinner with a sad shake of the head.

*   *   *

Our position had been compromised. The soldiers had been careless, lulled into complacency by my presence among them, perhaps. There had been too much activity out front of the house, too much smoking, too many cell phone calls, too many cars.

Mortar rounds landed close, spraying the upper floors with shrapnel. A sniper had fired at the outhouse. Things tightened up. There was a sense that something was building, as if a lighthearted moment had passed. Talk began of an enemy offensive, and the Ukrainian units were on high alert—more troops in the trenches, more patrols. The frequency of artillery attacks by both sides increased. Russian drones were constantly flying overhead. Daniel said there weren't enough vehicles for a retreat, and if the Ukrainians had to pull out of Pisky, it would have to happen by foot.

On my last day in Pisky, enemy artillery had a bead on our house. A bombardment of 152 mm shells thundered outside like Godzilla was stomping around. Within the cellar, it was the first time I saw the soldiers react nervously to the shelling outside. They moved away from the walls and sat on the floor. Some even put on their body armor. The walls shook, dust raised, plates and cups rattled on shelves.

A true artillery barrage, when the enemy is zeroing in on your position, is a terrifying thing to endure. It is, I imagine, like being strapped in on an airplane going down. You are helpless; survival is entirely out of your control. You sit there, looking into the eyes of the man across from you as the ground shudders and things fall off the walls and you hope, hope beyond hope, that it will just end. Those few moments of stone flat silence between each explosion are the most desperately hopeful you have ever lived. But then you hear the hope-crushing whistle of the incoming round, the high treble blast, the high-pressure concussion, the shaking ground, and then silence again and more hoping and more waiting. Until there's another shell, and another pulse of adrenaline. You inhale sharply at the top of your chest. The endless pulses of fear make you feel tired, like you have a cold. But you never panic. Panic is energetic, hyperactive. Or, panic can be freezing, paralyzing. Terror, on the other hand, is just fucking exhausting.

The atheists and agnostics start to seriously believe that the small talisman in their pocket might have kept them alive. Or maybe it was those pants they haven't washed for several days—they can't wash them now, of course. If anyone asks why, they just have to say, "for good luck." No one will ever criticize them for that. That is sacred ground, like talk about wives and children. Every time they walk out the door, the soldiers try to repeat, in every minute detail, what they did the time before in the hope that those patterns were what stood between them and the dark nothing.

Many soldiers were superstitious and carried objects for luck, such as woven angels or photos from home. Many wore crosses around their necks, or bracelets with Orthodox images. Some had a lucky bandana or a T-shirt. Some avoided taking a photo before they went out and never said goodbye.

You can die in the trenches or while picking strawberries from a garden. The war was omnipresent and everlasting. There was no escape except to build an imaginary distance between you and the war every day in your mind. To remember the person you used to be and not let the war become you.

Experiencing combat is nothing to be envious of, in terms of proving one's bravery. But there are few places with a greater concentration of philosophers than the battlefield. Late into the night, coal miners, forklift drivers, and teenagers sit around the table in the cellar talking politics, about the probability of God's existence, about love and family and what it means to lead a virtuous life. Like an impressionist's simple brushstrokes forming a masterpiece, simple sentences reveal profound insights born from experiences only a soldier can know.

Death sat on their shoulders every second of every day in Pisky. At first it was a weight to carry. Some grew stronger from the burden. Others broke. The enemy mercilessly reminded them that they could die today and that they will certainly die some day. In normal life, you find ways to forget this so you can be happy. In Pisky, soldiers embraced this truth. They laughed about it and went on living in spite of it. And they lived hard. War, above all, teaches you how much you want to live and how little that matters. All that counts are seconds and inches.

*   *   *

The morning I departed Pisky to return to Kyiv, I waited for Daniel in the courtyard of a shrapnel-shredded, abandoned home, but he never showed up. I assumed he'd been delayed by some military duty and didn't think much of his missing my departure, other than feeling a vague sense of regret for not having one more chance to shake the young man's hand and wish him well.

A day later, after I had returned to Kyiv, I got a slightly disjointed text from Daniel, explaining that he had been in a front-line trench the morning of my departure, and the enemy had attacked with mortars.

Daniel dove for cover, he wrote, just as a mortar impacted within the trench. His instinctual move, honed through months of what the Ukrainian soldiers called "natural selection" battlefield training, surely saved his life that day. The mortar shrapnel passed harmlessly overhead, but the blast gave Daniel what he called a "brain contusion." He said blood came from his ears and his nose, his ears were ringing, and he frequently lost consciousness.

Daniel was evacuated from the battlefield to a nearby military hospital. A few days later, his commander granted him leave to recover at home in Zaporizhia—only a three-hour drive from the front lines.

At one point, Daniel was stranded at a bus stop without any money. He texted me in a panic, and asked if I would wire some money to his bankcard. I sent him a few bucks, not thinking much of it. His effusive thanks underscored the selflessness of his military service—he couldn't even afford to go home on convalescent leave.

I had only known Daniel for a few days in person. But it was an unforgettable relationship, forged by our conversations in the trenches, or while sharing a cigarette during an artillery barrage.

I remember the day we first met. A group of us, about a half-dozen soldiers and me, were standing inside a cluster of farmhouses on a sunny day as the sounds of battle cut through intermittently. We all ducked at the sporadic Doppler zaps and supersonic pops of bullets passing overhead.

Zip, zap, pop, phew.

It almost sounded like birds chirping. Almost. So long as one forgot that each chirp was the lethal song of a trigger pulled with the intent to kill.

I was speaking in English to another Ukrainian soldier, wiping away beads of sweat from my forehead (whether due to the heat or the nearby bullets, I'm unsure), when a young man looked over at me with an expression instantly recognizable as a desire to talk. He introduced himself in English and said his name was Daniel. We talked for a while, dropping to the ground whenever the deadly chirping got a little too close for comfort.

Zip, zap, pop, phew.

"It is the DNR army shooting at us," Daniel said, looking to the sky in the direction of fire. "The separatist Russian army."

"So, this is… this is Pisky," he added after another flurry of bullets, smiling and laughing like he had delivered the punchline to a joke.

Daniel's fellow soldiers gave him the *nom de guerre* "Mobile Phone," because he was always taking photos with his cell phone. While I was in Pisky he ruined that phone, shattering the screen when he dove to the ground during an artillery attack. He was going to ask a friend from back home to send him a new one, he said, explaining that his hometown friends had also sent him his uniforms, body armor and first aid kit. The rest of his equipment came from civilian volunteers. The government only gave him weapons and ammunition, he joked.

ST. JOHN THE BAPTIST PARISH LIBRARY
2920 NEW HIGHWAY 51
LAPLACE, LOUISIANA 70068

Daniel told me how much he wanted to go home to Zaporizhia. He also talked about how hard it was to kill, and how it was even harder to see his friends die. He explained, revealing an understanding of human nature remarkable for a 19-year-old, that he did not hate his enemies. He thought many of them were probably just fighting for their friends like he was.

As a journalist, whose job it is to remain impartial in war, it was a challenge maintaining moral relativism toward those trying to kill me. Yet Daniel, a 19-year-old combatant, seemed to understand with an ease that eluded me the universality of duty. He didn't take combat personally.

Daniel said he had joined the military to defend his country from what he considered to be a Russian invasion. He called it a "real war." He had only been on the front for two months, but he had seen combat almost every day since he arrived in Pisky. Like many Ukrainian soldiers who volunteered after the war began in spring 2014 (Daniel was part of the Karpatska Sich volunteer battalion, which was later integrated into the regular army's 93rd Brigade), he had only a few weeks of training before leaving for the front. Most of his training occurred in combat. To stay alive, he shadowed the older, more experienced soldiers, learning lessons they had themselves learned the hard way. And when he saw others die, he would learn from their mistakes, too.

Like many soldiers, Daniel was superstitious. He had frequent brushes with death, and there was ultimately no explanation for his survival that made more sense than the crucifix bracelet on his wrist, or the letter from an elementary school student that he kept tucked in the front pocket of his body armor. Or the phone call he made to his worried mother, Marina, every day.

Daniel was committed to the war but confessed he was tired. He was worried about the psychological toll of the endless combat and wondered if he had seen too many terrible things to ever be a normal young man again. He feared that at 19 his spirit was already ruined for life.

"I want to go home, just for a bit," he said. "Just for a week."

"Do you get tired of the battles?" I asked.

"Physically, no. Morale, I'm tired. Very tired."

We spent nights around the dinner table as the artillery thundered and gunfire crackled outside the basement. We traded stories of home, of women, of my time as an Air Force pilot and his time on the front lines. I played the unwarranted role of mentor to a younger man who knew more about courage and sacrifice than I ever would.

Daniel had a lot of questions about life in America.

"What is Thanksgiving?" he asked.

"What are the beaches like in Miami?"

"Are the women in Los Angeles pretty?"

"Do they really wear cowboy hats in Texas?"

His dream, he told me, was to go to America. That's why he studied English so diligently. He liked American rock and rap music and knew the Hollywood action movies by heart, frequently dropping quotes by Schwarzenegger, Willis and Stallone. "Get to the chopper," he would say in a German accent before going on patrol, quoting Schwarzenegger's line from the movie "Predator."

Yet, unlike the action-movie actors he could quote, Daniel truly knew about war. And he knew it wasn't like in the movies. Daniel, more than many soldiers twice his age, recognized the things he would have to carry for the rest of his life because of what he had seen and done at the doorstep of manhood.

"You have no second chance here," Daniel told me. "If you get injured, it's just you and your medical kit. And nobody will help you, only you."

Daniel knew war was not black and white. And that is, I believe, why the things Daniel had done and seen in war haunted him so much. He saw his enemies as humans. Yet he never failed to pull the trigger. Consequently, he told me the war had "ruined him" and his "understanding of life." He said it would have been better for him if he had gone to war when he was an older man.

"I want to get out of these battles," he told me on that sunny day in Pisky. "I want to forget it. But I can't."

* * *

Daniel and I traded texts, emails, and phone calls during the several weeks of his recovery in Zaporizhia. I could sense a change in him from the introspective, yet ultimately optimistic, young soldier I had first met in Pisky.

He adopted a resigned fatalism, almost treating it as a matter of course that he wouldn't survive the war. Yet, there were things that lifted his spirits, too.

Although he didn't talk much about it, he said it was comforting to be back home around his mother. Returning to one's mother is often a confusing experience for many soldiers, particularly young men. The protective bonds of childhood, from which you tried to distance yourself as a measure of your manhood, become so intensely comforting. War teaches you to appreciate your parents' love more than ever before. I imagine Daniel felt something similar on his first trip back home from war, especially since he'd gone straight from living under his parents' roof to the front lines. Daniel's transition from childhood to adulthood occurred under artillery fire, where one can never complain about injustice, the entitlements of others, or life not being fair. His was an education with no room for failure, and without mercy.

As I settled back into life in Kyiv and Daniel recovered from his wounds, we talked about him coming to America. I promised I'd take him to a baseball game and that we'd visit the white sand beaches in Florida. He had a cowboy hat he liked to wear into battle. I recommended he bring it.

"The girls will love it," I promised.

He invited me to come visit him at home in Zaporizhia. I said I'd like to, but I had a lot going on in Kyiv. I promised him I'd visit next time.

After a while, as the prospect of returning to war began to loom over him, Daniel told me he was thinking about leaving the military. He was tired of war, he confessed. He'd like to go to university, he said, maybe even in America.

For a few weeks, we talked almost every day. And then our communication suddenly went dark. I regret now that I didn't reach out to him then. Life was moving fast for me in Kyiv. My reporting from the front lines had received a lot of attention, and I was enjoying the fact that my career as a journalist was finally going well. Now, looking back, I wonder what Daniel was going through at that time. The young man was likely torn between his desire to move on with his life and the gravitational pull of the war, which he couldn't escape.

Near the end of July Daniel sent me a picture over a text message. He was in his uniform, a half-cocked grin spread over his round, tan face. A wall pockmarked by bullet holes framed the background. He was back on the front lines, he wrote me in the attached message. He still had the headaches, he said, and wasn't totally recovered. But he needed to be back out there.

"It's my duty," he wrote me.

A mortar killed Daniel Kasyanenko in Pisky on August 6, 2015. He was 19 years old.

*   *   *

Two years later, I visited Daniel's parents at their home in Zaporizhia. At first, I suggested meeting at a café or a coffee shop. But Marina and Konstantin would have none of that and insisted I visit them at home.

The Kasyanenkos' old Soviet apartment building was nestled within an urban landscape of overgrown curbs, split pavement, and paint-peeling facades. Ukrainians have a habit of taking their shoes off at the door, which is what I did as I entered. Inside, the apartment was pristine, modern, renovated with new furniture, fresh paint on the walls, and a clean, unscuffed floor. There was a flat-screen TV in the living room and a computer with internet in the den. The living room used to be Daniel's bedroom. They gave their son the biggest room in the house, Konstantin told me with a smile. Now, there was a large L-shaped couch against the wall, and, on that day, a dining table crowded with many trays of home-cooked food and bottles of wine and vodka. A framed photo of Daniel sat on top of a nearby bookshelf.

Wrapped around the picture frame, I recognized the white Orthodox crucifix that Daniel had kept tied around his wrist in combat.

"It was hard for him," Marina told me over the opulent lunch she and her husband had prepared to celebrate my visit. "I didn't want him to go to war. But he was determined—he had to be the one to go."

In the weeks he was at home to convalesce in July 2015, Daniel was left with a ringing in his ears and he had eyesight problems due to his head injuries. His mother offered to take him to see a doctor, but he demurred. And, recognizing the other, invisible ways the war had wounded her son, Marina also offered to take Daniel to see a psychologist. He didn't want to do that, either.

While Daniel napped on the couch one afternoon, Marina quietly regarded her son. His hair was cut short, as was his habit, he was tanned and his hands were rough and calloused with dark spots left behind from healed cuts and scrapes. Marina put a hand on Daniel as he slept. Sleeping, he was like the boy she remembered. But, when awake, Marina could fully take stock of how much her son, her only child, had changed after going to war. There was a particular conviction, now, in the way Daniel carried himself that hadn't been there before. She also sensed a sadness when he talked about the war, or avoided talking about it.

"He came back as a different person," Marina explained. "He went to war as a boy and came back as a wise old man."

Daniel was still a volunteer soldier with no contract. He didn't have to go back. But, no matter what his parents said, Daniel was intent on returning to the front lines. So, rather than push their son and potentially send him back into combat on bad terms, they took him shopping. They bought him new military fatigues, special shoes and a watch. Then, before Daniel left, Marina tried one last, desperate time to change her son's mind.

"Stay here," she begged. "You're too young to have suffered so much."

"Mom, I have to go back," Daniel replied. "I have to go back to my friends."

* * *

As a habit, Daniel called his mother almost every day from the war. Usually, they didn't talk about anything important. But he was a young man who had gone straight from living under his parents' roof as a boy to living amid the death and danger of trench warfare as a young man. There was no basic training, no military academy; no time at a firing range, even, to serve as an interlude. It was like a jump cut in a film—straight from boyhood to war.

And so, probably for both Daniel and Marina, those daily phone calls were a way to dull the trauma of skipping all those steps in between that make sending a child to war a little easier, if such a thing is even possible.

"We were in touch every day," Marina said. "If he didn't call, we were in a panic."

When Daniel called his mother from the front lines on August 6, 2015, it was a day like any other. But something Daniel said struck Marina as extraordinary. Amid the shelling, the mortars, the rockets, the tanks and the snipers—he was complaining about mosquito bites.

Marina told her son to be safe. Daniel said goodbye and not to worry. And that was it. It was 10 a.m. when mother and son last talked on the phone. At 5:30 p.m., Daniel died.

For some reason, the next morning Marina didn't check the Facebook page for Daniel's unit, as was her habit every morning. At 10 a.m., a soldier arrived at the door. At the very first knock, both Konstantin and Marina feared something was wrong.

They opened the door and there stood the soldier.

"Are you Daniel's parents?" he asked.

They said yes.

"There is no Daniel anymore," he said.

*   *   *

There is no way for a parent to fully recover from losing a child. You can see that truth in the way the pain of losing Daniel is now, and may forever be, the bedrock to both Konstantin and Marina's lives.

The smiles, the jokes, the good times. That is all a thin veneer over the piled-up strata of pain and sadness that now reach straight down to the center of their souls. I saw that very same demeanor in Diane Foley, James's mother, when I met her in Washington.

When she spoke of her son, Marina's eyes frequently welled with tears. She kept going, anyway, and always finished what she had to say. Konstantin, at the sight of his wife crying, always stood and went to the kitchen, or another room. He didn't explain why. He just got up and walked away.

Maybe, you thought, he's too proud to cry in front of a guest. Especially an ex-US Air Force pilot who was friends with his soldier son and had been in the war with him. But the better you knew Konstantin, the better you understood that he wasn't trying to hide his sadness from you. He simply hated the helplessness he felt and so he stood, out of reflex. He moved in a direction, any direction, hoping that maybe there was something, anything he could do to make this pain stop. To end his wife's agony and the unspeakable quantity of regret that weighed on him for losing his boy, his only child.

But there was nothing to do. No action to take, other than to endure the unendurable. The moment passed. Calmed, collected, Konstantin came back and sat down and took a shot of vodka, and we went back to talking like before. One time, as Marina explained how Daniel liked to watch American action movies as a little boy, Konstantin left the room again. A moment later, he came back with Daniel's military uniform blouse in his hands. Konstantin stood proudly as he explained what all the patches and medals meant. Sadness now morphed into a father's beaming pride for a son who had embodied the thing that every man secretly hopes he possesses—courage.

*   *   *

My dad once told me that the true measure of a life well lived is to gain many years of experience, rather than simply repeat one year of experience many times.

If I had one more night at that dinner table in Pisky to share a meal and clink glasses with Daniel, knowing what I know now, I would tell him to be proud that he had crammed more experience and wisdom into each one of his 19 years than most 60-year-olds have achieved over a lifetime within safely repeatable circumstances.

As each year passes and the anniversaries of Daniel's death roll by, I hope to look back and have the satisfaction of knowing that each successive year was never wasted; that I have accumulated years of wisdom and progress, and have not simply resigned myself to endlessly repeat a year of disappointed hopes and broken dreams.

Winter 2015: Fighting for Freedom

The Old Man at the End of the World

Since returning from Pisky I felt like I'd been carrying a secret. Like Pisky was some dark message hidden in a secret pocket that I couldn't let anyone see. My mind was still in the war zone and would be for some time to come. I saw the war everywhere I went and in every person I met. I had become the living cliché of shell-shocked. Hypersensitive, for weeks I would instinctively duck to the ground at any loud bangs, like when a door slammed. My senses were extraordinarily aware of the moment I was in, yet my mind was trapped in the cage of where I had just been. I saw the world through the lens of the question, "How could things be like this with a war still going on?"

When you're in the war long enough, you're bound to start feeling that way. You have a limited roster of emotions you can take to battle, even if you're only a journalist, and so you drop the ones that aren't useful to your survival. Fighter pilots call it "compartmentalization." But, it's those unnecessary emotions that make you any good at writing about war. When war is new to you, you see it as something epic, maybe even romantic. But war becomes boring after a while. No, that's a lie. Combat can become ordinary, even routine. That's true. But that's not the real war. Real war doesn't happen until much later. Real war isn't about the bullets and the bombs and the blood. Even though that's what most people think. Real war is that hollowed-out feeling inside of you when you're back at home. It's that peace to which you return, but can never find.

War had clouded my vision like sunspots, distorting everything I saw in the pale light of peace. Nothing looked the same. I suppose that's what war does to you. It changes you so much inside that you think the world has gone and changed on you, too, while you were away. You can never go back to seeing things the way you did before. Yes, I was out of the war, but my mind was still in it. And war is one hell of a place to be.

It was time, four years since my last trip, to head back to the Himalayas.

Now, war had lost its mystery. I had experienced trench combat, tank battles, heavy artillery barrages, snipers, rocket attacks… real war. Consequently, I knew much more about war now than I ever had as a pilot. I now knew the smell and taste of combat, not just the look of it. My education occurred in the trenches and tank battles of eastern Ukraine. And I didn't forget about that Taliban rocket in Afghanistan.

But, after four years of constant motion, I felt as if I had gone nowhere. I had accumulated years of experiences, yes, but what did they amount to? I treated each day as a stepping-stone to something better. But what? Was I becoming addicted to war? Was I on the path to my inevitable destruction, or was I accumulating an education that would one day pay dividends?

I was still in search of something; that was clear. And, once again, I thought I could find it in the mountains. I'd thought that by returning to the edge of the world, there was a chance I could finally extinguish my attraction to war. But the truth was, war had become my home. Peace was the exception.

*   *   *

Distant from the sultry tan horizons of New Delhi, the Himalayan landscape surrounding the Indian city of Leh looked like a painted-on backdrop to a movie set. There was no horizon here, only a ragged panorama of barren, earth-tone peaks against the deep blue sky. At an elevation of 11,500 feet, the air was thin, crisp and cool. But the sun, with less atmosphere to filter it, was baking hot. One went from shivering to sweating simply by stepping out of the shade.

I had come to Leh with plans to visit a 53-mile-long lake called Pangong-Tso, which runs along the Himalayan border between India and China at an altitude of about 13,500 feet. It was a long, difficult trip to get there, and for the journey I hired a jeep with a Swiss traveler named Franz. An older man, graying and balding, Franz had the solid frame and weathered features of someone who had been on many adventures. That was enough for me to trust him as a traveling companion.

As we left Leh and ascended into the mountains, the road often dissolved into a barely discernible line in the rocks and gravel, winding its way over steep mountain faces and across arid, high-altitude valleys. Unlike the forested, glaciated Himalayas in Nepal, these mountains were bare rock with scarcely any snow on them save for a random dab here or there on the highest peaks. It was the starkest and most otherworldly terrain I'd ever seen.

Immediately out of Leh, the road passed through small villages and beneath ancient Tibetan palaces and temples teetering on impossibly steep cliffs and ridgelines. After an hour, we left the Indus River valley and climbed toward the Chang Spa pass, which topped out at 17,688 feet, roughly the same height as Mount Everest base camp in Nepal.

On a small saddle of flat ground at the top of the pass, we passed an Indian army camp where soldiers were sent to acclimatize to the altitude before deploying to defend the Himalayan border with China. Since the 1962 Sino-Indian War, India has remained in a de facto conflict with China over unresolved border disputes in this rugged region. As evidence of this unspoken, forgotten conflict, we passed through a network of Indian military outposts along the route to Pangong-Tso. The troops' presence in those lonely places—practically the only evidence of humanity—felt ominous and familiar. On the faces of the Indian troops I recognized the look of men enduring difficult circumstances.

The road to Pangong-Tso, like many in Ladakh, was constructed and maintained by Tibetan refugees pressed into construction gangs by the Indian government since the 1960s, following China's invasion of Tibet. Small troupes of Tibetan road workers, comprising both men and women, were constantly at work in some of the harshest conditions imaginable. They kept India's Himalayan roads clear by removing rocks deposited by landslides, or filling in potholes—all by hand, mind you. Those poor souls endured a lonely and miserable existence. They lived in small encampments made of old parachutes perched on what little flat ground there was to be found at those heights. There were no trees for shade and no water except for the rare trickle of snowmelt.

It did not escape me that this grand adventure of mine was the daily reality for these people, and a multigenerational purgatory for the Tibetan nation in exile as a whole. One of those workers, a young man, smiled, clasped his hands as in a prayer and nodded to me through the jeep's window as we passed. How little we had in common, I thought, and what different circumstances had led our paths to cross for that brief, shared moment of eye contact.

The road tacked down from the high passes into severe valleys of rock and scree. All at once, it seemed, we rounded a corner and poking through the hall of mountains before us was the burning-blue surface of Pangong-Tso. It was like the mountains ahead were a curtain drawing open, revealing more and more of the lake as we approached it. A few minutes later and we were on its shore—the highest saltwater lake in the world.

Like a hypercolor ribbon dividing India from China, Pangong-Tso is 53 miles long but only about three miles across at its widest point. The opposite shoreline, that of China—that's to say, occupied Tibet—was totally uninhabited. The water was a collage of turquoise and aquamarine shades of green and blue; the colors were so vibrant and clean, it was like standing within an airbrushed photo. The thin air at high altitude does something special to light. Distances disappear and colors glow unnaturally brilliant.

The only settlements along the lakeshore were a small collection of tents and shacks at the north end called Spangmik, and some seasonal tents and a half-dozen primitive homes farther east at a place called Man. They were both on the Indian side of the lake. A few gazebos on the shoreline, too, but that was it. Otherwise, it was pure wilderness—the unmerciful end of the world.

We stopped for a while at Spangmik for lunch. The Tibetan girl who served my meal of rice and yak meat giggled at me and boldly tussled my blond hair.

Franz laughed. "You're a rock star," he said in his songful Swiss German accent.

After lunch we pressed down the shore to Man and chose to spend the night at the home of an old Tibetan man and his wife. They rented out rooms to travelers and welcomed us warmly.

After we had settled in, the old man made Franz and me tea and served us *tsampa* as we sat under a parachute tent and watched the dancing ripples of wind cut across the surface of the lake. Sitting there, I told Franz about my time in the military and my reasons for leaving that life. He said nothing at first. Then he told me that his wife had recently died, and he had decided to spend the rest of his life traveling.

"Don't forget how exciting it feels, right now, while it's all beginning," Franz said. "It all goes by so fast," he added a moment later, his voice trailing away with the wind.

*   *   *

After tea, Franz went to take a nap and I joined the old Tibetan man and his wife inside their home. A CD playing the Buddhist "*om mani padme hum*" mantra set to music was endlessly looped in the background. A shrine to the Dalai Lama, draped in a white *khata* scarf and with offerings of fruit laid out before it, occupied a shelf over the main table.

The old man, whose name was Tsering Tunduk, wore age-worn clothes and a black fedora and his face was darkly tanned and weathered into a rough, leather-like hide by a lifetime in the high-altitude sun. He also wore a necklace with an intricately woven amulet, which he handled like a priceless work of art.

Short but solidly built, Tunduk stood straight and moved purposefully. His 66-year-old body and features had been hardened by a difficult life, not broken by it. The old man smiled constantly and used his hands a lot as he spoke, placing a hand over his heart to show sincerity, and a hand on your shoulder or knee for rapport. He pulled on his wispy Fu Manchu mustache when speaking seriously, as he did when he said in his halting, staccato English, "I came here because it reminds me of Tibet. It's a very hard life here. We live like nomads, as my parents did."

Tunduk used to graze cows, but not anymore, he explained. The extended periods spent outside in the harsh climate around Pangong-Tso became too demanding as he grew older. In the winter, when the temperatures sometimes drop to -40 Celsius, his cheeks and the tip of his nose would turn black from frostbite. Now, he grows barley and black peas, the same crops his parents tended in Tibet when he was a boy.

Only about two miles of water separated the old man's home from Tibet. Tantalizingly close, but Tunduk had not set foot in his homeland since 1959.

"I'm still waiting for freedom," he said, smiling, as was his habit no matter how sad the subject. "And when Tibet is free one day, I will walk back home from here. I will try my best."

Nine families permanently inhabited Man, and Tunduk was the only Tibetan among them. He married his wife, Ganyen Tsultime, who is a native Ladhaki Indian, on December 10, 1989—the same day the Dalai Lama received the Nobel Peace Prize. Tunduk was very proud of that fact.

Tunduk and his wife led a Spartan life in Man. They stockpiled food, fuel, and other supplies for the winter in case snow closed the roads. Dried saucers of yak and cow dung layered the top of their roof. That dung was used to fuel the stove, as there were no trees for firewood. The old couple slept, ate, and passed time in the main room, where the stove provided both cooking heat and warmth for the whole house.

As we talked on that night, I noticed a faded old picture on the wall of Tunduk as a young man. In it, he wore US army fatigues and stood beside a much taller, Caucasian soldier in the same type of uniform.

Curious, I asked Tunduk about the photo.

"That was my friend from the CIA," he told me as he peeled potatoes in preparation for dinner. He nonchalantly added, "When I was a soldier in the Indian Army."

Naturally, my interest piqued.

I asked Tunduk to tell me his story.

He agreed.

"But first, let's eat," he said, smiling.

* * *

Tunduk grew up in a village in an area called Nangchen, in the Kham region of Tibet. His father had been the village boss when the Chinese invaded in 1959.

When the Chinese soldiers arrived in Nangchen, they hauled Tunduk's father and mother into the town square for the *thamzing*, or "struggle session"—a public spectacle used to humiliate, torture, or execute Tibetans who opposed Chinese rule. The soldiers tied Tunduk's father's arms and legs behind his back, beat him, and shot him in the head. Next, they painted a bullseye target with charcoal on the chest of Tunduk's mother. With ropes, the soldiers suspended her by the arms from two wooden poles. They used her for target practice, continuing to shoot long after she was dead. The Chinese soldiers made Tunduk and his younger sister, Khunda, watch all of this.

"I cried, and my sister cried," the old man told me quietly through the dim light. "There was nothing left to do but cry."

Tunduk remembered looking into the faces of the Chinese soldiers and seeing nothing. Neither pleasure nor pain. It was as if they had no emotions, he said. A lifetime later, when the old man closes his eyes to sleep he's still haunted by images of his dead parents. As he described their murder, Tunduk's usual smile was replaced by something cold and expressionless. His mind was back in a time and place that no words, not even from one's native tongue, have the power to faithfully recreate.

"I wanted revenge," Tunduk said. "I wanted to kill them all."

His face, turned to me then, was empty. I saw the unmistakable look of a soldier in the old man's eyes.

Orphaned and alone, Tunduk and his sister joined a group of refugees for a treacherous two-month-long journey across the Himalayas into India. It was 1959, the same year the Dalai Lama fled to India as an exile. Along the way, over the high mountain passes, the two orphans faced hypothermia and frostbite, starvation, and persistent attacks by Chinese troops. Tibetan freedom fighters escorted the refugees across the mountains, saving their lives. For Tunduk, the image of those brave men leading their people to salvation shaped the rest of his life.

* * *

After China invaded Tibet in 1950, a grassroots resistance movement rose up across the Himalayan kingdom. By 1956, tens of thousands of Tibetans were fighting an insurgency against Communist China's occupation. These bands of guerrilla warriors ultimately coalesced into a resistance army called the Chushi-Gangdruk, which translates to "Four Rivers, Six Ranges," signifying unity among all the regions of Tibet. Chushi-Gangdruk freedom fighters played a key role in the Dalai Lama's escape from Tibet in 1959, and they led armed escorts for the tens of thousands of refugees who followed in their exiled leader's footsteps to seek sanctuary in India and Nepal.

Wielding swords and World War I-era weapons such as British.303 Lee-Enfield rifles, the Chushi-Gangdruk fought the modern, mechanized Chinese army on horseback. Though badly outgunned and outnumbered, the Tibetans' fighting spirit and small successes eventually caught America's attention. The CIA began an operation in 1957 to airdrop supplies and train handpicked fighters as paratroopers at secret bases in Saipan; Camp Hale, Colorado; and Camp Peary, Virginia—the CIA's training facility known as the "farm." These Tibetan commandos embarked from secret air bases in East Pakistan— what is now Bangladesh—and parachuted into Tibet. Special U-2 spy plane flights provided intelligence about the geography of inner Tibet, much of which was still uncharted in the 1960s.

By 1962, however, the CIA's Tibet operation was in limbo. The Kennedy administration, skittish from the botched Bay of Pigs invasion, questioned the utility of the mission and the risk it posed to a budding rapprochement between the US and India. But the political calculus for both the US and India changed on October 22, 1962, when China attacked India along its Himalayan frontier. In response, Indian Prime Minister Jawaharlal Nehru turned to the US to help stand up an all-Tibetan combat unit for the Indian army, tapping into the CIA's existing recruiting and training networks used for the Chushi-Gangdruk operations.

India's CIA-backed, all-Tibetan mountain warfare unit was code-named Establishment 22. Its original purpose was to use Tibetans' genetic ability to perform at high altitude to wage a guerrilla war against China in the Himalayas. But the 1962 Sino-Indian War cooled before the Tibetans could be trained and fielded. Recognizing the unit's potential, however, India deployed the all-Tibetan outfit to combat in hot and humid East Pakistan in 1971, and later in the Himalayas to fight against Pakistani forces.

The CIA's Tibetan operation was never more than an annoyance to the Chinese, and many of the Tibetan fighters were either killed or captured. Ultimately, US airdrop support for the Chushi-Gangdruk guerrillas continued until President Richard Nixon's normalization of relations with China in 1972. Yet, India's Establishment 22 was never disbanded. Based in Chakrata, Uttarakhand, Establishment 22 is now called the Special Frontier Force and continues to serve along India's Himalayan border and in counterterrorism operations. To date, the unit has never officially faced Chinese soldiers in combat.

*　　*　　*

When Tunduk fled Tibet, he was a 14-year-old orphan unable to communicate by means other than hand signals. His options were limited as a refugee. At that time, India was conscripting many Tibetans into road construction and repair teams for the country's Himalayan highways. That life didn't appeal to Tunduk for many reasons. Above all, he wanted revenge. His hatred for China was absolute. The choice was clear—the angry orphan boy would become a soldier. (For her part, Khunda, Tunduk's sister, had settled in Simla, India.)

In 1969, ten years after watching Chinese soldiers kill his parents, Tunduk volunteered for Establishment 22 and began six months of basic training. (The old framed photo on his wall was from that time.) He saw combat in East Pakistan in 1971 and fought in a 1986 battle on Siachen Glacier against Pakistani troops in which 17 Tibetans died.

"The army gave me a good life," Tunduk said. "But… sometimes, I became frustrated when I had to fight in other people's wars. Our aim was to fight with China. Pakistan is not my enemy. China killed my parents and captured my country. China is my enemy."

As a devout Buddhist, Tunduk believed he was a sinner. He had killed in combat and was deeply ashamed of it. To atone, he lived a quiet life at the edge of the world on Pangong-Tso lake. It was a place that reminded him of Tibet, and where, as an old man, he could live the peaceful life he never knew as a boy. To put the past to rest, he'd found a new home—a process with which I was well acquainted.

I asked Tunduk about the amulet he wore around his neck. He told me it was a gift from the Dalai Lama, given as a token of appreciation for his military service. Now, that small talisman attached to an old, frayed piece of yarn was the old man's most prized possession. It symbolized the most wonderful treasure of all—to not be forgotten.

"The Dalai Lama is my God and my king," Tunduk told me. He held a hand over the amulet. "I still believe Tibet will be free. I still have hope that I'll go home one day."

He paused, pulled at his mustache, and then added, "But not without the Dalai Lama."

No matter how impossibly different my path through life may have been from Tunduk's, for one evening we were able to sit together at a table as friends, share a meal, laugh, and tell stories about our lives as soldiers.

That night after dinner, as the roof timbers creaked in the Himalayan wind, Tunduk played cards with a neighbor. The radio was on, tuned to Indian news. The newscaster spoke about the war in Afghanistan. My war.

"I see these things, and I know what those people are going through," Tunduk said to me. He put a hand on my arm. "We had our dark times, too."

At dawn the next morning, the old man stood outside his home on the lake shore, thumbing his prayer beads and chanting, "*om mani padme hum*." His mouth moved almost imperceptibly as he repeated his mantra. The light of the sun grew slowly from where it would rise, behind the mountains of Tibet on the opposite shore.

The old man's eyes were fixed across the burning blue water toward his homeland, from which he had been exiled for more than half a century. The impossibly far-away seemed close enough to touch in the thin air. Right there, just across the water, a life and a world that no longer existed. A yesterday that seemed so close, but was gone forever.

Later, with the jeep loaded and Franz patiently waiting to go, Tunduk and I sat together on yak hides atop a low wall outside his home, sipping on butter tea. I felt like I didn't want to go, not yet. But I had to.

Tunduk watched the sun climb over his forbidden homeland across the lake.

"We are all the same in our hearts," he told me. "We want to be happy and to not suffer. We all believe in the same God; we just have different techniques."

The old man gave me a tight, long hug goodbye.

Freedom Isn't Free

Simply asking a freedom fighter why he or she fights is usually less than illuminating. They are frequently so nonchalant about what they've done that their explanations fall short of any sort of meaningful revelation. Yet, their humility offers an insight into their motivations. Above all, they fight because they believe it is their duty.

About two months before a mortar killed him, Daniel Kasyanenko told me: "We are fighting for our home and for our land. Ukraine is a free country, and when Russia invaded I had no other choice. I had to fight."

Four months later, and thousands of miles away from Ukraine, 77-year-old Jampa Choejor offered me a cup of masala chai at his home in the Jampaling Tibetan refugee settlement outside Pokhara, Nepal. I was still slightly amped from the motorcycle ride it took to get from Pokhara to Jampaling—an hour-long slalom course dodging cows and overloaded buses on the free-for-all chaos of Nepal's rural roads.

As we sat with legs folded on yak-skin blankets while sipping our tea, Choejor, a former Buddhist monk, explained why he renounced his monastic vows in 1959, joined a Tibetan guerrilla army and went to war against Communist China.

"When the Chinese came, they raped women, they bullied, they killed," Choejor said. "There was no freedom, no religion. After so many brutal acts, there was no way to stay silent. We had to fight. We couldn't stay living like that."

Choejor fought in the Tibetan resistance until 1974, when the Nepalese military routed the Chushi-Gangdruk guerrillas out of their mountain hideouts in the remote Mustang region on the border of Tibet and Nepal. Now Choejor lives in poverty. His worldly possessions comprise some threadbare clothes and a collection of old framed photographs of the Dalai Lama.

"We suffered in Mustang during the resistance," he said. "But there was no other choice. The Chinese were killing so many people and things were getting so bad, we had to fight back."

* * *

I've spent a lot of time with both Ukrainian and Tibetan freedom fighters. Distant in time and space, these two war stories are connected by common threads, including this: when faced with the invasion of their homelands, many ordinary Tibetans and Ukrainians voluntarily took up arms and went to war.

"We're fighting for freedom against Russia because they want to keep us under their control," a 21-year-old Ukrainian National Guard volunteer soldier, who went by the *nom de guerre* "Grizzlo," told me from a trench outside the front-line town of Shyrokyne in April, 2015. Machine-gun fire crackled in the distance, as did the occasional mortar blast. I flinched frequently and instinctively at these sounds of war; Grizzlo never did.

"They want to take us in their control and we don't like it," Grizzlo told me, cradling a Kalashnikov in his arms. "We are a freedom country and we are Ukraine and not some land of the Russian Federation."

Kelsang Tsering, 82, a former Buddhist monk who fought with the Tibetan resistance from 1955 until 1974, told me something similar when I asked him why he went to war.

"I saw what China was doing in Tibet and it made me so angry, I had to fight," he said.

Tsering and I talked over the kitchen table in his home in the refugee settlement in October 2015. A flickering fluorescent lamp lit the room, and a picture of the Dalai Lama draped in a white *khata* scarf was on the wall. Tsering's wife sat on the floor, legs folded, spinning a prayer wheel while she chanted a Buddhist mantra.

"I'm still very angry," Tsering said, smiling paradoxically. "But I'm in no position to fight, I'm too old. My thinking is that the younger generation has a responsibility to secure our land. If I see young Tibetans fighting each other, I tell them the real enemy is on the other side of the mountains. If you're really brave, go fight the Chinese."

*　　*　　*

For many of the Ukrainian and Tibetan freedom fighters I've met, their decision to become a soldier wasn't really a decision at all. Their country was invaded, innocent people were dying, and so they had to fight.

It's simple arithmetic. It's not romantic or idealistic, although to an outsider it seems that way. Their decision to serve was no more under their control than a balloon in the wind. They reacted to the injustices to which they bore witness the only way they possibly could—by fighting back.

"I don't think I've accomplished something big, but I feel satisfied," said Lopsang Chombel, 84, a former Tibetan monk who took up arms to help the Dalai Lama escape Tibet in 1959. He went on to serve with the Tibetan resistance in Mustang until 1974.

"I did everything honestly and truthfully when my country needed me," Chombel added conclusively.

"It's impossible not to be motivated when the enemy has attacked the motherland," 53-year-old Ukrainian volunteer soldier Vasiliy Ivaskiv similarly said as he cooked me breakfast in a basement artillery shelter in the front-line village of Pisky in eastern Ukraine.

Ivaskiv, a former coal miner from the western Ukrainian town of Ivano-Frankivsk, called me "America" and had a habit (despite my protests) of using his body to shield me from sniper fire. Compact and muscular, he exuded energy, leading day-long patrols with men less than half his age. A father figure, he always seemed to be fixing something and usually did the cooking for the younger troops.

"When I was working in the mines, we could tell who was a good worker by how much he ate," the old soldier said as he heaped food onto my plate. "So eat up."

Ivaskiv volunteered to serve in the Ukrainian army after he had made a few trips to deliver supplies to front-line troops in the early days of the war. "I saw those young men fighting and dying for Ukraine, and I knew I had to fight too," he told me, proudly adding that his father had fought the Nazis in World War II.

When he left for war, Ivaskiv said he had to step over his wife, who was in a sobbing heap in the doorway. She begged him not to go.

"There was nothing she could do to stop me," he said. He scooped some scrambled eggs onto my plate, then paused and stood before me with the pan in has hand for a moment before he added, "I had to go. It was my duty."

* * *

Similar to their shared reasons for volunteering to go to war, Tibetan and Ukrainian freedom fighters' moral certitude about the justice of killing parallels an absolute commitment to the cause of defending their homelands.

"We have to fight them here because they won't stop," a 28-year-old Ukrainian sniper named Volodymyr told me in Pisky. He used to work at an Obolon beer factory and had a wife and young child back at home. He believed that if the Ukrainian army left its positions in the Donbas, Russia's forces would keep advancing, maybe going as far as his hometown in the West.

"I never hesitate to shoot," he said. "And I never feel regret."

Back in Nepal, I asked Choejor how he made the mental leap from life as a Buddhist monk—for whom all killing, even of insects, is forbidden—to being a soldier who had killed Chinese soldiers in hand-to-hand combat.

"In the beginning, I was thinking we were monks, and so we shouldn't kill," he explained. "But when I recalled all the abuses, all the terrible things the Chinese did, I forgot my hesitation to killing. After seeing so many bad things, I forgot that killing was a sin. I was hoping to kill, and I felt happier the more I did it."

"I felt no hesitation to kill," Tsering similarly replied when I asked him about killing.

"The Chinese were killing our own people," he went on. "For the sake of our country and our own people, I did not hesitate at all. Fighting back was the right thing to do."

*   *   *

At face value, heroism is illogical. Darwin, in particular, was consumed by the idea. It went against his thesis that the ultimate aim of any living creature is to survive and pass on its personal set of genes. What then, motivates a hero to purposefully risk his or her own life for the chance that someone else's genes might survive? It doesn't make sense within the narrow calculus of natural selection.

Of course, humans are not natural selection automatons. There's a lot more that goes on deep inside our craniums than a lifelong devotion to advancing our DNA. We are also shaped by the incomprehensibly complex, and often illogical, impulses of our emotional selves, which sometimes inspire us to tread to the edge of death out of a sense of duty.

Consider what Choejor told me about his time at war.

"We never thought about retreat, we were totally prepared to die," said the monk who became a freedom fighter. "We thought, 'We were born here. If we have to die, then we will die here.'"

We can't all be heroes. Our species couldn't survive if we were. Uncommon heroism and common cowardice are our species' survival mechanisms. That's why, in a moment of crisis, most people stand idly on the sidelines while the heroic few step forward.

Heroes are the keel that keeps the sailboat of humanity from tipping over against the force of our own selfish instincts. After years of reporting on war, I know I'm not a hero. I'm equipped with the standard-issue stuff of human DNA. But I tell heroes' stories. After all, only the unheroic can write about war well and honestly. Heroes, for their part, never think what they're doing is all that heroic. And they don't go looking for opportunities to be heroes, like we war correspondents sometimes do. Heroes, by their nature, don't appreciate how rare and exceptional they are. They are typically nonchalant about throwing their lives on the line to save a comrade, or their willingness to endure months, even years, of suffering and violence to protect people they'll never meet.

Heroes, among their many qualities, are a breed of people who never judge their personal actions based on what others would or would not do. They understand, instinctively, what is right or wrong, and the only formula they apply to their actions is a sense of duty. Fairness, privilege, entitlement, jealousy—none of that factors in. It's simple. They see an injustice and they want to fix it.

*   *   *

The day I first arrived in Ukraine in August 2014, I visited the Maidan, Kyiv's central square and the epicenter of the 2014 revolution. Bullet holes still pockmarked the sidewalks and street signs at the top of Institutskaya Street where pro-regime snipers had gunned down protesters the preceding February.

When I visited, the area was covered in beds of flowers and candles, which surrounded framed photographs of the more than 100 protesters who had been killed. The faces of the fallen included the young and old, men and women. As I walked around, trying to appreciate what had happened there six months earlier, I heard an American voice, which stood out from the Russian and Ukrainian ones.

"Freedom isn't free," that voice said.

I thought about those words almost eight months later as I stood on an artillery-cratered beach in Shyrokyne and spoke with Ivan Kharkiv, a 20-year-old journalism student who had volunteered to fight with the Ukrainian National Guard's Azov Battalion.

"Peace is possible, but Ukraine must be a free country," Kharkiv said. "We must free our territories and then we can live in peace."

Freedom isn't free.

I was still thinking about those words when I met Tsering Tunduk at his remote, lakeside home in the Himalayas.

"Every being has a birthplace, a place where they dream of going back to," Tunduk told me. "My identity is Tibetan. Until death we will want our country back."

Freedom isn't free.

I've met many people over the years whose lives symbolize that truth. Like Oxana Chornaya, a 37-year-old university professor who put her life on hold when the Ukraine war began so she could deliver supplies to Ukrainian troops on the front lines. She wore body armor over her floral sundresses as she weaved an old, fully loaded minivan through artillery fire.

"Sometimes I'm so afraid I can't take my hands off the steering wheel," she confessed. "I get so scared. My knuckles are white and I can't breathe. But I have to do this," she added.

Freedom isn't free.

And Lhasang Tsering, 68, a former Tibetan guerrilla fighter who served in Mustang. He turned down an opportunity to attend medical school at Johns Hopkins University to join the Tibetan resistance—a decision for which the Dalai Lama personally scolded him.

While Tsering was in high school in India, a Reader's Digest story about the Tibetan resistance in Mustang had inspired him to be a soldier. He explained: "I said to myself, 'Good God, these guys are fighting, and if we younger Tibetans don't fight, how will the resistance continue?'"

Tsering now lives in Dharamshala, India, where he owns a bookshop called "Bookworm." But, even after all these years, Tsering's commitment to Tibet's independence hasn't wavered.

"In my view, achieving freedom comes first," he said proudly. "I decided then that I was going to dedicate my life to the freedom struggle. And I am still ready to die for independence."

The price of freedom is usually set by those who try to destroy it. Yet, despite the Russian tanks and the Chinese pogroms, Ukrainians and Tibetans still believe freedom is worth the fight. Perhaps freedom simply means more to people who have experienced the alternative.

I asked Chombel if he would ever go back to Tibet. The 84-year-old former monk and freedom fighter immediately and flatly replied: "Not without the Dalai Lama."

He added: "If I go back before Tibet is free, it's a kind of surrender. If I were younger, I'd go back and fight. But I'm old and will die soon, and now it's up to the younger generation."

Freedom isn't free.

Those words and what they truly mean echoed in my mind on August 7, 2015, when I received an email from a French journalist, informing me that a mortar had killed my friend, 19-year-old Daniel Kasyanenko, on a battlefield in eastern Ukraine.

"I remember he told us that war is a bitch and that he wanted to go home," the journalist wrote. "Bloody war. Although we know he's a soldier and that can happen, sometimes it's really unfair... he was just 19."

Freedom isn't free.

The Nangpa La

To show what Tibetans were willing to endure for freedom, in November 2015 I hiked across the Nangpa La. I went alone and without a guide.

A remote tentacle of the ancient Silk Road trade route, this mountain pass over the Himalayas, connecting Nepal and Chinese-occupied Tibet, tops out at more than 19,000 feet. Up until 2008, merchants herded their laden yaks across the Nangpa La's glaciers to deliver their goods in Nepal. Meanwhile, stealthily flowing within the yak trains was an undercurrent of Tibetan refugees, as many as 2,000 to 3,000 a year, who escaped China across the high Himalayas, seeking freedom in Nepal.

After China invaded Tibet in 1950, the Nangpa La became the most frequently used escape route for Tibetans fleeing Chinese occupation. An underground railroad of human smugglers concealed haggard and wayward Tibetan refugees in safe houses and in monasteries before they could be spirited down the mountains under the cover of darkness. The refugees' goal was to reach the U.N. Human Rights Council office in Kathmandu, where they could claim asylum without risk of Nepalese agents deporting them back to China to face certain imprisonment, torture, or even execution.

China suspected the Nangpa La was a lifeline for the Tibetan resistance movement and pressured Nepalese authorities to crack down on the flow of refugees. Those efforts reached a peak in 2008 as unrest simmered in the Tibetan Autonomous Region in the run-up to the Beijing Olympics that summer. China didn't want scenes of protest from Tibet stealing airtime from their choreographed spectacle, and so Beijing clamped an iron fist over Tibet. Reprisals against the families of refugees were swift and brutal. Many abandoned their hopes of escape.

Today, Nepalese troops and an undercover police network collectively maintain a dragnet for Tibetan refugees in Nepal's Khumbu region. But hardly any more refugees come that way anymore. Armed Chinese troops now patrol the Nangpa La under the watchful gaze of high-tech surveillance cameras. As if the Nangpa La's high altitude, frequent avalanches, daily storms, Arctic cold, and treacherous paths were not lethal enough, Tibetan refugees now have to add gunshot wounds to the myriad ways in which they could die on their path to freedom.

Some obstinate traders, however, attempted to keep crossing the pass for the first year or two of the Chinese crackdown. But the tight monitoring network and the harsh prison sentences doled out to violators proved effective deterrents, completely stemming the flow of both refugees and traders.

During my first trip to the Khumbu in 1998, Tibetan traders' tents covered the center fields of Namche Bazaar. They laid out their goods on exotic carpets, I remember. It was an eclectic market of knock-off mountaineering clothing, yak-wool blankets, meat, jewelry, and Buddhist talismans. By 2011, however, when I returned to the Himalayas fresh from the military, the Tibetan yak trains and their gold-toothed, ponytailed drivers were all gone. The trading places in Namche Bazaar were empty. And, unknown to me at that time, the hidden flow of refugees had vanished, too. Since 2009, the annual number of Tibetan refugees to reach Nepal dropped from 2,000 to 3,000 down to around 200, with none coming across the Nangpa La.

*   *   *

The way began along the Dudh Khosi valley up to Namche Bazaar on the same path I had taken toward Mount Everest twice before. After Namche Bazaar, however, I deviated from the typical trekker's route. Instead of following the Gore-texed flocks heading northeast toward Everest, I turned west and traveled up the less visited Bhote Khoshi River valley.

As I went farther and climbed higher, the Alpine forests thinned into meadows and shrubland. I first stopped in 12,467-foot-high Thame, a village long known for its spectacular Buddhist monastery perched on a ridgeline hundreds of feet overhead. Unfortunately, the monastery and much of the village had been leveled in a magnitude 7.3 earthquake that May, the second of the two massive earthquakes to hit Nepal in 2015.

In Thame, I met a 58-year-old Italian mountaineer named Lorenzo Gariano who was leading an international effort to rebuild the village's lone school. A veteran of many Himalayan expeditions, including successful ones to Everest, Gariano had been visiting Nepal since 2001. Consequently, he understood how China's closure of the Nangpa La had affected life in the region. Not only had the flow of refugees been thwarted, he explained. A linchpin for the area's economy was now gone. "Nothing's ever been the same," Gariano said.

From Thame, I hiked over a ridge to the nearby village of Thame Teng, or Upper Thame. Gariano had told me about an old artist named Pasang Nuru who lived there with his family. Nuru, as Gariano recounted, had lost his fingers to frostbite crossing the Nangpa La during his escape from Tibet many years ago. Now, he was one of the region's most renowned artists. Needless to say, for both the sake of the story and my own curiosity, I wanted to meet Nuru.

Once in Upper Thame, I canvassed the trailside shops asking if anyone knew where the artist Pasang Nuru lived. I was met by mostly blank stares. It was clear that part of the Himalayas received fewer foreign trekkers than the route to Everest. Ultimately, one old woman selling yak-bone prayer beads by the trail pointed me to a home high up the hillside.

I asked, "Pasang Nuru?"

She smiled and clasped her hands together as in a prayer.

I weaved through many yak grazing plots, all separated by waist high-stone walls, to reach the home. I knocked and a girl, maybe 10 years old, opened the front door.

"Namaste," she said.

"Namaste," I answered, bowing respectfully. "Does Pasang Nuru live here?" I asked, just trying out some English for the heck of it.

"Yes, he's my father," the girl quipped back in crisp, British-accented English.

The door opened wider, and the girl's mother stood there, appraising me. I offered a gift—a box of Snickers bars I had picked up that morning—at which both of them smiled. The mother showed me in, draping a white *khata* scarf over my neck after I had dropped my fully laden rucksack by the door.

Inside, sitting beside the stove, was Pasang Nuru. He stood and smiled and put out his two fingerless hands to shake the one I had thoughtlessly extended, as a welcoming gesture.

He sat me down and asked me some questions about my journey while his wife served us tea and Tibetan bread. He was a mild, excessively polite man. With thinning hair, a wispy mustache, and a particular way of nodding with every cluster of words, he spoke like he was gently sending them across the air to me. Nuru wore a knock-off North Face down jacket over his slight frame, and, as Gariano had explained, he was missing all his fingers. We talked for several hours, and over that time I was able to piece together his amazing story. Nuru's daughter, incidentally, served as an interpreter for the times his English failed him. She was studying English in school and was already quite fluent. As recompense, she had some questions for me about dinosaurs, which I tried my best to answer.

Pasang Nuru Sherpa, then 64 years old, used to be a nomadic trader from the Tibetan town of Tingri. He had lived through the 1959 Tibetan uprising and the hell of China's ensuing campaign of retribution. During that nihilistic orgy of violence and destruction, of the 6,000 Buddhist monasteries in Tibet before 1959, only 370 survived until 1960.

Nuru had wanted a new life inside Nepal free from communist oppression. As a trader who had been back and forth to Nepal, his eyes were open to what life was like outside the Orwellian police state Tibet had become under Chinese rule. Nuru wanted out. So in January 1975, when he was 23, he decided to cross the cross the Nangpa La and never return. But a storm threatened to end that new life before it had a chance to begin. The snow fell until it was up to Nuru's chest and he couldn't go any farther, trapping him above 19,000 feet in temperatures 30 degrees below zero Celsius.

"The weather is very dangerous on the Nangpa La," Nuru explained, rubbing together the remnants of his hands. "I had to sleep on the pass. I had not eaten for a week, and I was very, very cold. I thought I was going to die."

Nuru continued to rub his ruined hands together as he looked past me, toward a memory he was reliving without a way to explain it.

"It was very cold," he said at last.

Nuru survived the storm, but he spent the next year in and out of hospitals, ultimately losing all his fingers and toes to the effects of frostbite. Handicapped and unable to continue his livelihood as a trader, he later defied his injuries to become a painter—and a successful one to boot.

I told Nuru about my plans to cross the pass, and he told me not to go.

"No Tibetans come across the pass for more than four years," Nuru said. "The Nangpa La has always been dangerous, but Chinese soldiers are there now, and they shoot you for trying to cross."

He paused for emphasis, then added, "It is not worth it anymore."

In that instant I thought back to the conversation with my dad years earlier.

"You're going to get yourself killed for a story that no one cares about," he'd warned.

Nuru's wife made us a meal and we ate together. Then we said our goodbyes and I was on my way again.

*   *   *

The arid Bhote Khoshi River valley opened up with the miles to reveal more and more of the snow-capped peaks lining the border with Tibet to the north. I encountered hardly any other trekkers, but I walked past a procession of lonely Buddhist *chortens* and *stupas*, some hundreds of years old and many in ruins from the earthquakes. These relics marked my way.

The last outpost before the truly wild Himalayas was the tiny settlement of Arya. It was nothing more than a cluster of stone huts and yak pastures at an altitude of about 14,000 feet. After Arya, I didn't see another person for a week.

The hike along the Nangpa La refugee route, the old Tibetan trade route, was not easy. I felt fine and strong, but the weight of my pack took its toll, and the altitude often left me short of breath. I carried, among other things, a tent, sleeping bag, gas stove, clothes, food, first aid kit, crampons, and a DSLR camera. Nights in the tent were bitter cold, and the effort of hauling a heavy pack at those altitudes was tiring. But the corporal excesses of easy living melted away with the miles and the altitude. And what was left became something harder. Blisters became calluses. A sunburn turned to tan. Sore muscles became stronger ones. My body hardened to the task as the days went on.

The trail was rough, meandering, and at times hard to identify. This ancient, nomadic route had faded into the wild terrain after years of disuse. Plus, landslides from the two earthquakes in 2015 had wiped out some sections of the trail, leaving me no choice but to skirt along steep, crumbling cliffs in places. You can only hope the shifting ground will support your weight as you nervously peer down hundreds of feet of exposure. A fall would be fatal. Even if you survived the tumble, a broken leg or ankle would likely be a death sentence in this remote section of the Himalayas.

Intermittent clues to the path's history sprang up along the way. Nomads and refugees had built stone huts and walls as shelters from the wind at various points. At these abandoned campsites I found disintegrated sneakers with the soles worn through, along with tattered jeans and T-shirts. I also found a shattered porcelain vase with Chinese lettering. Yet, there were no other active signs of human existence. It was complete, abandoned isolation.

Every night I set up camp in places where the rock provided shelter from the wind. As the sun set and the temperatures went with it, I would heat water, which I had collected from snow or small streams along the way, to cook my oatmeal and brew my instant coffee.

At night in the tent when the wind died down, the silence played tricks with my mind. I imagined footsteps outside, even voices. It was not natural to be so alone and cut off, and my mind imagined these things to fill the void of human interaction that I, whether I knew it or not, so desperately desired. Once or twice at night I called out, "Who's there?" I even sprung from my tent at one point with my small knife in hand, ready to defend myself from the bandits, or the Yeti, which I had so surely heard creeping around the tent.

Of course, I was totally alone. However, what I did see, once I had calmed down from my night terrors, was the most impressive night sky of all my life. The Milky Way shimmered like the phosphorescent nighttime wake of a ship across the sea. The mountains were now only black zigzags framing the bottom of the sky. There was no wind, then, and the silence was so absolute I could hear my own heartbeat. I felt, for the first time, like I wasn't traveling through this place, but that I was a part of it. I could almost feel the sky above passing through me like an electromagnetic field. Or maybe it was just the cold.

Over the following days, as I hiked farther and higher, it was, in fact, quite eerie to have this massive place all to myself. I was lucky with the weather. The days were perfectly clear, giving all the colors a supernatural radiance highlighted by the clarity of the thin, high-altitude air. Looking beyond the peaks that reached as high as jetliners fly, I could see the dark blue sky begin its fade to black.

"Through footless halls of air ... up, up the long, delirious, burning blue," I found myself reciting, recalling familiar sensations of altitude and freedom as I approached the pass and the Chinese border.

Still, a grounding reality marked my time in the mountains. During the cold nights and the hard work of each day's walk, my thoughts often drifted to the hungry, tired, and scared Tibetan refugees who had accomplished the same journey in jeans and tennis shoes. How they must have suffered. They didn't have my fancy mountaineering clothing, a tent, or a portable stove on which to cook hot meals. They hiked at night, fearing Chinese border patrol troops who shot on sight. Unable to use flashlights, the refugees linked arms so as not to lose each other in the darkness. They used socks for gloves. Duct tape held together their disintegrating footwear. During the days, they tied strips of black trash bags over their eyes to protect from snow blindness.

I wondered if this untamed landscape and its proximity to the heavens had inspired the Tibetan refugees to wax poetic like I had. More likely, however, their eyes and minds were firmly planted on the rock and ice beneath their freezing feet.

What incredible things people do, and what endless suffering they are willing to endure for freedom.

It's true, freedom isn't free.

It's worth everything.

Gravity

Lumde, Nepal
November 11, 2015

So here I am, once again plodding up into the Himalayas, straining against the weight of my pack, the incline of the trail, the diminishing power of my legs and lungs with the altitude, and the gravitational pull of the life I left below. I've spent the four years since I was last here as a war correspondent in Ukraine, Afghanistan, and Iraq. Is war where I now belong?

I wrote before that the mountains do not solve any problems, they only create newer, simpler ones. It is a chance, for a moment, to pretend the burdens of everything you left behind don't really matter. And truly, nothing does matter up here except for the simple chores necessary for survival.

You focus on the trail, food, water, blisters, the aches and pains of the miles, where to sleep, what clothes to put on to stay warm, what things to stuff in your sleeping bag at night to have warm in the morning. These myriad decisions, which require no more complexity of thought than a caveman's, relieve you from more complicated, civilized distractions.

Yet, all the while, this simple existence gives you such a spiritual and intellectual reprieve that it launches your creative and introspective talents into an orbit impossible to achieve in normal life. You realize that what you always suspected was possible, is.

That is the attraction and the addiction to this place and this existence. And as a writer, it's a place where I feel most capable of achieving something bordering on proficiency with my craft.

There is typically a singular goal on these trips into the mountains, fixed in place over your thoughts like you're chasing the moon. Last time I was here it was climbing Island Peak. Now it's the Nangpa La.

Those challenges, and the unknown ability of my body to meet them, funnel my thoughts, focusing them like light in a lens. They are a grand goal, which justifies the hard work by giving me a sense of meaningful purpose, which otherwise eludes me.

It is also, of course, tragic when the goal is achieved. Success, in the end, is the most deflating of all outcomes. You realize, only then, that your worries were unfounded. Your physical and mental limits have not been reached. You become aware of the untapped potential still within you, locked away by your fears.

You can only hope that there is enough time left in this life to find out where that horizon truly lies.

On this trip, I have placed that shifting horizon on the Nangpa La. After tonight, I walk off the edge of the world. And I truly have no idea what to expect.

I wonder if the trail will be passable—did the recent earthquake wash away the fragile slopes I need to cross and climb? Will the nights be too cold? Will I stay healthy in the altitude? What if I get hurt? Will I be strong enough to reach the pass? I also wonder if this journey will produce a story worthy of what I risked to be here.

I'll know the answers to those questions weeks, months, and years later as I reread these words. The only evidence of the anxiety and the uncertainty I now feel will be in these pen strokes, bold today, but surely to be faded by new worries and new joys over time.

For now, my mind and soul live here in this stone hut high on a Himalayan ridge. The sun is setting and the clouds have moved in as they so often do in the late afternoon. The evening wind is shifting the timbers of the roof. The air inside the lodge smells of smoke from the stove. I am warm and happy here. A plate of Tibetan *momos* and a mug of hot chocolate are in front of me.

My thoughts are pointed up toward the Nangpa La, where the answers to my questions and the closing pages of this chapter of my life are waiting for me. But as I have learned with any trip, the ultimate measure of the distance traveled is not to be taken at the destination, but upon one's return home.

I go to find
What has, I fear,
Only existed in my mind.

I toil, work, suffer and strain
Pushing on to a height
Where one cannot live,
Nor life itself
Dare remain.

All for what?
I cry for explanation.
For glory, fame, respect, or even admiration?

Or, is it to close an end...
for which the journey
Is my one true, and only friend.

* * *

When I reach the top of the pass, there's nothing there. Only a new mountain vista and a dark sky overhead. I touch foot in China but go no farther. If there are Chinese cameras watching, or Chinese troops ready to shoot, I never see them. As far as my senses can tell, it's just another high mountain pass where the air is cold and thin. I think, briefly, about going farther and testing my luck. But I have no energy for it, and it all seems sort of pointless and silly, anyway. I wonder what I'm even doing there. What is this story about? Am I really trying to tell the world about the forgotten plight of Tibetan refugees, or am I simply submitting myself to another bout of pointless suffering in search of salvation?

From the top of the pass, I take a long look into the arid, forbidden plains of Tibet. Then, I turn around and begin the long walk home. But, like the thousands of Tibetan refugees who had passed this way before me, I have only a direction, not a destination in mind.

2016: Taking the War to the Enemy

The Sound of God

I hiked until it grew dark. Clouds moved up the valley, flowing toward me like a floodwater until I walked into their leading edge. In the dark mist my visibility reduced to the few feet in front of my face. According to my map and my memory, I was not too far from the nearest village. But I had to stop. Or else I was likely to step off a cliff during my blinded wandering.

The narrow space between two huge boulders on a patch of level ground offered some shelter from the wind. I pitched my tent in between the rocks and fell asleep easily and deeply. The next morning dawned clear. I packed and was on the move before eating anything. A few hours later, I stopped at a lonely hut where a curious Sherpa couple offered me pancakes and coffee. By lunchtime I was back in Thame, where I had stopped before setting off for the Nangpa La.

A week outside of civilization with no human contact. A week that had almost returned me to something forgotten inside myself. I wasn't cured yet, but I wasn't thinking about war, either. I was dreaming up more stories I wanted to write in the Himalayas and other wild places. More mountains to climb, more passes to cross.

In Thame, I sat down to an omelet and an Everest beer. Then, some British climbers told me about the terrorist attacks in Paris at the Bataclan night club. It had happened while I was on the Nangpa La.

A week later I was on a plane bound for Paris. Home, wherever that was, would have to wait.

*   *   *

I arrived in Paris late at night, still bearded, thin, and sunburned from the mountains. On the cab ride in from Charles de Gaulle airport the radio commentator talked about a cultural civil war in France. Another war. A natural condition from which there was no escape. Both for us as a species and for my life, it seemed.

Paris was lonely and cold. A friend of my father's had given me the keys to his apartment for as long as I wanted. With no pressing financial constraints to limit my time in the city, I settled into a routine. It was a historic moment in Paris, and I was happy to be there to write about it all. But I was tired. I had been without a home for too long, immersed in war after war, writing about heartache and loss.

On Thanksgiving I ate alone at a French café while reading George Orwell's *Homage to Catalonia*. A call home to my parents that evening was, in the end, more a reminder of my isolation than anything to celebrate—very different from the thrill of calling home on Christmas Eve during that first trip to the Himalayas as a 16-year-old.

Paris had been home, once. The place where I had lived for two years as a graduate student at the Sorbonne, just after graduating from the Air Force Academy in 2004. My dream, for so many years, had been to return to Paris as a writer. But now that dream seemed flat. Paris wasn't the same. Or, maybe, it was the young man who dreamed of living here who had vanished along the way.

Now, I was a traveler with no home, a vagabond collector of experiences leaving a breadcrumb trail of memories to nowhere. But no matter how unique, marvelous, or profuse your life's experiences might be, they can only be thoughtfully considered, and therefore pleasing, if you have a home to which you can return. Otherwise, you are a bumblebee, helter-skeltering from one impulse to another, traveling a long distance, but going nowhere. A life lived for experience is full of sensory pleasure, but it's not a happy one. Not truly. A happy life has both pleasure and purpose. All those experiences you amass must be useful in some way for you to feel any real, lasting joy from them.

Otherwise, each journey is just another sugar rush, energizing you for a moment before it disappears, leaving you flat and tired. I didn't realize it at the time, but I was living from one hit to the next. I needed to find a home. My mistake was in thinking that home had anything to do with geography.

I returned to Ukraine in the middle of December. I went back to the front lines a few times, but a familiar restlessness quickly set in and I was ready for a new story. So, in the spring I decided to go to Iraq. It was time to return to my war.

*   *   *

Like in Ukraine, the transition from peace to war came quickly in Iraqi Kurdistan. In less than an hour by car, I went from the glitzy shopping malls and fast-food restaurants of Erbil, Iraqi Kurdistan's capital city, to front-line forts where you worried about chemical weapons attacks and the possibility of being beheaded or burned alive if taken prisoner.

The morning of my first trip to the front lines outside Mosul, I had an omelet and a pain au chocolat along with an Americano coffee. In my hotel room, as I packed for the days ahead, I flipped between CNN International and BBC World News on the TV. Then, with some time to kill, I went to the gym. There was a bowl of fresh apples and a cabinet of water bottles on a table by the door. The gym was on an upper floor, with broad windows looking across the Erbil skyline. It was air conditioned, cool, with brand new weights, treadmills and elliptical machines. Later, after showering, I had lamb kebab with grilled vegetables for lunch in an outdoor terrace surrounded by olive trees. I sent a few emails, did some reading, and then it was time to go to war.

At the appointed hour, my fixers—Khasraw Hamarashid and his twin brother, Xoshnaw—arrived at the hotel in a silver SUV. They had a polished Kalashnikov stashed up front and Khasraw kept a pistol tucked in the back of his trousers. Both men were Kurdish *peshmerga* soldiers. A volunteer fighting force, the *peshmerga* represent an ancient warrior tradition dating back from the time before Alexander the Great. In Kurdish, the word, *peshmerga,* roughly translates to "one who faces death." Today, this ancient warrior caste is under the command of the Kurdistan Regional Government, an autonomous region in northern Iraq.

Minutes later we were out of the city. Fast-food restaurants on the roadside gave way to goat herders and their flocks. This land's ancient rhythms still beat beneath its modern surface. We drove through the first Kurdish police checkpoint where the guard waved us through with little hassle. My companions' father was a *peshmerga* colonel, and family connections are a priceless commodity in this culture. "Ameriki," Khasraw said, nodding toward me in the back seat. The guard smiled and gave the Kurdish greeting; a raised hand, palm out, flipped back at shoulder level.

We traveled south and then west, heading toward the southern flank of the *peshmerga*'s front lines surrounding Mosul. We passed through a rolling landscape of wheat fields and eroded hills. On the side of the road, only a couple miles from the front lines, I saw a father helping his son onto a horse. They were alone in a field. A moment later we passed a fire-scarred section of the road framed by eroded trenches on either side.

"Daesh took over this area in 2014," Khasraw said, using the pejorative Arabic nickname for ISIS. "Most of these people fled. But when we kicked Daesh out, they came back." After a pause, he added, "Life goes on."

The sky was clear, which filled me with relief. ISIS likes to attack when it's cloudy or raining, Khasraw explained. The terrorists knew AmericanUS warplanes were less effective at snuffing them out in bad weather. But on clear days there was no hiding from theUS warplanes and drones. For that reason, as we raced along a long, straight road toward the front lines outside Mosul, I was thankful for the blue skies above.

Along the Gwer front, where we were headed, ISIS had a history of using chemical weapons. Mustard gas, in particular. Yet, among the *peshmerga* troops I visited, none had gas masks or protective suits. They only had a few bottles of bleach with which they planned to douse themselves if ISIS used chemical weapons. Apparently, an Iranian news report had claimed that pouring bleach over your skin was an effective way to neutralize the effects of mustard gas. I was more than a little dubious about the efficacy of this technique, but, out of deference to my hosts, kept my mouth shut. Apart from the chemical weapons threat, attacks otherwise typically comprised mortars, and sniper fire. Suicide bombers were the biggest threat.

Being on the front line with the *peshmerga* was like going home. The gallows humor, the way a meal became a solemn bonding ritual, the smiles interspersed with the distant, vapid stares of memory flashbacks. The sounds of mortars and gunfire, the butterflies when danger approached, the exhilaration when it receded. The names of the people and places had changed, but the war was all the same.

The *peshmerga* snipers would take potshots at the ISIS militants we could sometimes see across no man's land. But they never hit anything while I was there. At night they opened fire into the black abyss of no man's land; red tracers raced away and then seemed to slow and float down in the distance. Silence in between bursts of bullets. Except for the casual conversations of the *peshmerga*, or the metal clanking of more rounds being loaded. It was all just a remix of what I had felt in Ukraine.

Near sunset, I was on the rooftop of a *peshmerga* fort in Gwer. I stood beside a *peshmerga* commander, General Omar Hama Ali Farag. We watched together as ISIS militants scurried between their positions a mile away across a dry riverbed. On the other side of no man's land, the terrorists looked like distant rats with their all-black garb and frantic movements. There they were. The black-clad foot soldiers of the terrorist army responsible for so much death and destruction. Disciples of the same twisted group that had brutally killed James Foley.

Small in stature, with a trimmed salt-and-pepper mustache, Farag wore a black and white turban and the Kurdish *sal u sepik* uniform—a traditional outfit with a thick waist sash over a loose-fitting tunic. The general paced back and forth among his men with his hands clasped behind his back. At times he had a fatherly air. In other moments, which coincided with the thumps of airstrikes, Farag's eyes narrowed and his face transformed into a remorseless expression I have only seen among soldiers in combat. Then, as we peered across no man's land, jet noise roared overhead. I looked up and saw the arrowhead shape of two F-16s scorching across the clear blue sky.

"That's the sound of God," the *peshmerga* general told me.

Farag, like many older *peshemerga* soldiers, had survived Saddam Hussein's al-Anfal genocide in the late 1980s. More than 180,000 Kurds died in the attacks, which included chemical weapons dropped from Saddam's fighter planes. The sounds of jet engines had thereafter stirred terror among the Kurds who remembered al-Anfal. Years later, however, the snarl of American warplanes inspired an altogether different feeling among the Kurds.

"Now the sound of the planes makes me happy," Farag told me "I can't explain how important the US planes are for us. If we can't hear the sound of the planes, we can't stay here and fight."

As the US fighter jets roared above, the *peshmerga* soldiers pointed to the sky, laughing and smiling. Empowered, a few soldiers fired potshots toward the enemy lines. The sun was low, and the sky was clear. The jets were clearly visible. Then, the thunder of bombs. Puffs of tan dust and smoke rose where the enemy had been. A flock of startled birds took flight. I felt satisfied. I thought back to my previous profession. I knew what war looked like from up there.

"*Allahu akhbar*," Farag said. God is great.

"*Allahu akhbar*," I agreed.

As the sun dipped below the distant, ancient hills, we stood together, listened to the sound of God and watched our enemies die.

* * *

After sunset, Farag directed me downstairs for dinner. We took off our shoes and entered a carpeted room decorated with the trappings of war. A Kalashnikov and a pair of binoculars hung on the wall. Weapons and ammunition were piled in the corner, including a Soviet-era rocket-propelled grenade launcher and a crate of warheads. A soldier performed *Salaat*, the Islamic prayer ritual, on a prayer rug set against the far wall.

In the center of the room, dinner was served on top of a plastic sheet—a spread of flat bread, tomatoes, barley soup, and fried potatoes. Around the meal, a dozen soldiers sat on the floor with folded legs. I took my place next to Farag, and as we dug into the food he apologized profusely for not serving any meat. The soldiers didn't normally have this much to eat, he explained, but they considered my visit to be a special occasion worth celebrating.

I thanked him for his hospitality and then presented a bag of gifts I had purchased from a grocery store in Erbil, which included a carton of Marlboro Reds, jars of peanut butter and Nutella, and a jumbo-size package of Nescafé Gold instant coffee. It was a modest offering, but I might as well have brought the moon based on the soldiers' overjoyed expressions of thanks.

"Before, we had no friends but the mountains," Farag said. He smiled and put a hand on my shoulder. "Now we have America, too."

Scenes like this have played out in these lands since biblical times. Warriors gathered around a meal, talking about life, love, politics, memories of the fallen, and the mystery of faith. I knew I was only a journalist, a journeyer and a witness to this war. But the *peshmerga* treated me as an honored guest. In their eyes I symbolized all of America. And as a former Air Force pilot, I was a human face to the sounds of the jets and the bombs, which continued to rumble outside as we ate.

Eager to take advantage of their guest's assumed omnipotence, the *peshmerga* soldiers peppered me with questions. They were especially curious about the upcoming American presidential election and which candidate would prove to be a greater friend to the Kurds.

For my part, I delicately broached the subject of past American missteps. Like why America had left the Kurds in the lurch after the Persian Gulf War when they rose up against Saddam, or why we did nothing to stop the al-Anfal genocide. The Kurds dismissed the shaky history of US support. They said the no-fly zones throughout the 1990s had allowed them to become strong as an autonomous territory. And they were grateful for the 2003 invasion to topple their nemesis, Saddam Hussein.

"We are in debt to America," Farag said, adding: "We will be friends with America forever for the help they've given us. We had the Anfal genocide and many sufferings, but the *peshmerga* have always seen America as our friend. We could have never gotten rid of Saddam without George W. Bush. And we can never have our independence without America's help."

After dinner, we had tea. Soldiers took turns using the prayer rug to perform *Salaat*. And then the room began to clear. One by one, soldiers gathered their weapons and headed to the roof. The last embers of daylight had faded and night had arrived.

At night, ISIS patrols and suicide bombers crept across no man's land to launch attacks. Consequently, the *peshmerga* soldiers kept awake and alert. They cradled their Kalashnikovs and scanned the pitch-black night for the enemy. The *peshmerga*'s lines were not continuous, with breaks of more than a kilometer in places. The intervening terrain was wide open with little foliage or natural relief for use as concealment. Consequently, ISIS used the night for camouflage.

Night-vision goggles were scarce. To compensate, the Kurds had strung light poles along the front, bathing the first few hundred yards of no man's land in yellow light. Beyond that was the void. The emptiness held nothing, but also all the dark imaginings that a mind could produce. If you stared into the dark long enough, you saw your fears manifest. The quarter moon's glow silhouetted two *peshmerga* soldiers standing on the roof of the compound. I reflexively jumped at the unexpected burst from their Soviet-made RPK light machine gun. The red tracers rocketed out and then seemed to slow down as they dipped toward the ground in the distance. Another gun joined in from a *peshmerga* position down the line, maybe half a kilometer away. The tracers were beautiful as they flowed across the black void of no man's land. There was some return fire, but I couldn't tell from where.

Then it was quiet again, and scary. I thought back to books I've read about the Pacific theater in World War II—classics like *Helmet for My Pillow*, and *With the Old Breed*. I remembered stories about nights on battlefields in Guadalcanal and Peleliu as US Marines took turns sleeping in foxholes, ever fearful of Japanese soldiers lurking in the dark ready to slip a knife into those who let down their guard. Fear similarly consumed the night in northern Iraq. The hours passed slowly until sunrise.

At daybreak, most of the *peshmerga* soldiers dropped into a relieved sleep. A few stayed awake to keep watch, but the first rays of the sun had washed away the fear of the night.

*   *   *

In the morning we visited another *peshmerga* fort about two kilometers away. To get there we had to pass through an unprotected stretch of the front lines. My companions, the *peshmerga* twins, drew their weapons and pointed them out the windows of the SUV as we accelerated. A *peshmerga* general had been attacked on this stretch of road just a week earlier. For our part, we made it without incident and minutes later I was on the new fort's roof chatting with Lt. Col. Bahaddin Qadir, the unit commander.

The morning was crisp and clear. On a balcony below us, a soldier was splayed out on a cot in deep sleep, immured from the world with a Kalashnikov and an RPG launcher propped beside him. Just a few days ago they were taking heavy sniper fire, Qadir explained as we rested our elbows on the parapet and peered across no man's land.

Snipers.

My heart sank. Snipers were a personal fear of mine. The mortars and the artillery I could handle. But snipers, well, that was different.

I thought about Ukraine and my close calls with the snipers there. I felt naked. My eyes darted back and forth along the low hills across the Great Zab River less than a mile away, where ISIS had established its lines. Every house, tree and boulder. Every crag, dip and rise. I imagined snipers everywhere.

I ask Qadir what had changed. Why could we now stand on the roof with impunity?

"The clear weather," Qadir replied. "Daesh knows the US Air Force is up there, watching. They're afraid."

Qadir said the coalition airstrikes had stopped ISIS dead in its tracks.

"Personally, I'm so thankful for the airstrikes," Qadir said. "I can remember having to hide from Saddam's jets. Now our enemy suffers the same fate. That makes me so happy."

A dog barked down below. A flock of startled birds took flight. Then the earth rumbled with a bass thud that felt like someone was blowing air in your ear. All four of us on the roof exchanged looks. Smiles reflexively crept across our faces. My feeling of nakedness at the thought of snipers gave way to a rebounding sense of empowerment. Jet noise growled overhead and then another boom, and another and another and another. A black mushroom cloud rose to the south. It looked like spilled ink.

Qadir rubbed his sleepy eyes and smiled. Then he leaned against the parapet with his back turned casually toward no man's land and said, "You know, we don't even need a salary. I say give our money to the US. Keep the bombs coming."

Evidence

Evil doesn't always reveal itself through goose-stepping armies or skyscrapers collapsing on a clear autumn day. Sometimes, it's only a sun-bleached bone in a field.

This was the place the old *peshmerga* colonel had wanted to show me. It wasn't anything special by the look of it. Certainly, this plot of brown grass on a hillside in northern Iraq was less striking than Sinjar's endless rows of pulverized buildings, blasted to bits by ISIS bombs and US airstrikes. But here on this plot of land, so easily overlooked, a few white bones and some tattered clothes melded into the earth. All that remained of 24 people. Men, women and children. Civilians. Murdered by ISIS. Their bodies left in the open to rot. Their bones picked clean by wild animals and burnt white by the sun.

It was one of about 100 mass graves in Sinjar. You probably wouldn't even notice the place if you didn't know to look for it. Yet, it was psychically radioactive. The evil and suffering that the ground concealed hummed and crackled, passing invisibly through the air, then right through you, turning you inside out, ruining you from within. You can't see it, touch it, or smell it. But you feel it. And there's a particular way the hushed voices of the dead echo to the living in a place like this. I've felt the same thing at Auschwitz, at the Babi Yar ravine in Kyiv, and at ground zero in New York City. Call it ghosts, spirits, something ethereal and fantastic, or maybe just the mind trying to reconcile the ordinary collage of senses with the intellectually putrid knowledge of what happened here. How could someplace so peaceful have been the epicenter of something so evil?

The hatred that leads people to do this to one another seems all the more extraordinary when you see its evidence in such an ordinary plot of earth. Whatever quantity of hate is required to kill scores of helpless people, the ISIS terrorists brought it with them. A vile seed brought from far away, sprouting in this blood-soaked earth. And what crime did the murdered commit? Nothing more than the accident of their births as Yazidis, Christians, or Shia Muslims. I went to Sinjar to see the true nature of ISIS. I wanted to stare straight into the aftermath of the terrorist army's perversion, regardless of the consequences.

* * *

Looming over the plains north of Mosul, Sinjar Mountain had offered a refuge to all those who had fled from the ISIS invasion in August 2014. Now, after years of bitter fighting, the Kurds had liberated the towns in the mountain's shadow. The civilians were back living among the ruins. But from the look of it, life was hard. Trash was piled on the roadside. The burnt-out shells of armored vehicles dotted the fields. Many damaged buildings remained abandoned. The overt military presence of the *peshmerga* and the fact that even shepherds had Kalashnikovs slung over their shoulders evidenced a society living on the contact line of peace and war. Often, the most jarring parts of war are the vignettes of normal life that coexist with the fighting. Ordinary scenes like children going to school that seem so extraordinary amid the backdrop of war. But those everyday images tapered off as we neared Sinjar. That place was a tomb. Lifeless like a bone-white coral reef.

ISIS took over Sinjar and the surrounding area in August 2014. A coalition of Kurdish and Yazidi forces freed the town in November 2015 after a tough, two-day fight. About 88,000 civilians used to live in Sinjar. By May 2016, the town's only inhabitants were the approximately 5,000 Kurdish soldiers deployed to defend the area from the ISIS militants still camped only about two or three miles away. No civilians were left living in Sinjar, and it wasn't hard to understand why. Total destruction isn't a phrase to use lightly. But in the case of Sinjar, it applied. There were no subtle hints about what happened there, only brash, bold statements that hit you like a Mike Tyson punch. No building was spared. Some had a wall or two caved in from the explosions. Most were reduced to piles of concrete rubble and twisted rebar. Endless, street after street.

Such a scene is for the eyes like listening to Mozart's "Requiem" is for the ears. It's multilayered and terrifying, simultaneously filling you with awe and making you want to weep. You can't turn away, and where would you look anyway? There's no eye to the storm, no blank, untouched quarter within which to rest your gaze and recover. The war's destruction is everywhere. The only escape is to close your eyes or just leave that place.

The *peshmerga* soldiers said the damage was due to both coalition airstrikes and a scorched-earth demolition campaign by ISIS. The Kurdish soldiers took us around town to see the destruction. ISIS militants had used underground tunnels to shelter from airstrikes, and they had carved out holes in the ground from which snipers would emerge like gophers to pick off *peshmerga* soldiers. ISIS turned the town into a gauntlet of booby traps and remotely detonated explosive devices. It sounded like one hell of a fight. And based on the flat expressions on some of the Kurds' faces, I understood the echo of the bullets and the bombs had not yet silenced. I asked about the mass graves, and Col. Shuqur Qasim Yusif took me to the place with the bones. The Kurds had discovered about 100 mass graves so far, he told me. There were likely more left hidden on the outskirts of town, Yusif added, but they were in no man's land and inaccessible.

Most of Sinjar's residents fled when ISIS invaded, becoming refugees. ISIS lined up and shot many of those who stayed. About 5,000 civilians died. The ages of the dead ranged from 1 to 70. Young women were spared for use as sex slaves. The words the Kurdish soldiers used to explain what happened here fell flat on my ears. I had no experience in life on which to draw to imagine such horrors. Only images from movies, or ideas from books I'd read. I'd seen dead soldiers before. A tragedy, yes, but the sight of dead soldiers doesn't sting like a genocide.

I tried hard to appreciate what had happened in Sinjar, I tried to feel it. But all I could muster was a detached coldness. I felt a stirring anger, and a feeling of camaraderie with the Kurds as we shook our heads in disbelief at the awful stories. Still, when I expected more, I felt nothing. The time to mourn and absorb the tragedy had not yet arrived. The vapid souls who had committed those terrible acts were nearby. They were still shooting rockets and artillery into the heart of Sinjar. Their suicide bombers were still making kamikaze charges across no man's land. The war was still there.

Later, after returning to Erbil, I went to a shopping mall. I wanted a normal afternoon with no war, a chance to pretend like I was back home. I wandered, stopping in stores that sold Levi's jeans and North Face hiking pants. I ate a Hardee's hamburger for lunch. It felt, for a moment, like I was back, a part of the main again. Like it was all a dark imagining and that shopping and eating in a food court could distance me from Sinjar by a thousand miles, not a six-hour car ride.

I was on my way to the exit when I noticed what looked like a flea market. Rows of tables behind which men, women and children were selling all sorts of knickknacks. Curious, I had a look. A tall young man wearing a *keffiyeh* was standing to the side. I asked if he spoke English. He did, introducing himself as Muhammed. We shook hands and I asked Muhammed what was going on. He explained that this was a bazaar for refugees to sell their goods and make a little money.

Thousands of civilians in Iraq and Syria had fled from ISIS. They'd found safety in Iraqi Kurdistan but were now without work, left living in tents in sprawling refugee camps. I roamed the bazaar with Muhammed. The women were dressed beautifully and smiling. The children played and misbehaved, to their mothers' exasperation. One young man sold wax candles. He introduced himself as Ahmed and said he was from Mosul and used to be a lawyer. Now selling candles was the only way to make a living for his wife and him. At a table, young women from Syria wore bright red cardigans and sold sweets and cakes. They smiled and giggled among themselves the way friends do.

I saw them all and felt happy. I saw the life, the smiles, the decisions to not give up and to keep on living no matter what. There were lots of broken dreams there, too; lots of hardship and pain locked away behind each smiling face. You might see a glimpse of it here or there in a forlorn, far-off gaze. But, mainly, there was a sense of happiness, of community. That mall could have been Anywhere, USA. The waxed floors. The soft rock piped over speakers in the background. The coffee shops, the fast-food joints, the American brands. It all felt so normal. But then I was with the bone in the field, again. My senses told me everything was okay, but my mind told me that wasn't true. My mind can't forget. I understood what those refugees at the mall represented. The war was still there.

I met two children, a brother and sister, both refugees from Sinjar. They were with their mother who wore a beautiful garment and was selling trinkets. We didn't speak the same language, but I said hello and the children smiled at me curiously before continuing to chase each other around the tables. Muhammed said something to the woman about me being an American and a journalist. She put a hand over her heart and said, "*Shokran.*"

The evidence that people are good at heart doesn't always reveal itself through grand gestures of charity or faith. Sometimes, it's only a young man or woman fighting for love, children playing, or a woman with a hand over her heart saying *thank you.*

Compartmentalization

Off the Syrian Coast
July 2017

The sounds of aircraft launching off the flight deck rumble deep within the bowels of the aircraft carrier. Conversations in the officers' mess room, where I'm having chicken cacciatore for lunch, dutifully pause while the jet engines above decks run up to full afterburner. Then, the walls and floor shudder when the steam-powered catapults launch the fighter jets at an acceleration of zero to 184 miles per hour in just two seconds.

Just by the sound of it, there's no way of knowing if each successive launch is for combat or for training. But there's a good chance the jet you hear is headed to war. Each day about 16 to 24 sorties launch from the USS *George H.W. Bush* en route to Iraq and Syria to support the coalition air war against ISIS, called Operation Inherent Resolve.

On this day in August 2017, as I intermix eating and interviewing, I sit across the table from an F/A-18 Super Hornet fighter pilot who goes by the call sign "Bacon." I ask how he defines success.

The pilot replies, "When you start seeing people going back to their homes, when we see cities being liberated, that's success."

A Navy lieutenant, Bacon is trim, articulate, and effusively polite. He sports a mustache to match his reddish hair. The mustache is a tradition among male pilots on combat deployments—the Air Force does it, too.

If Bacon wasn't in his flight suit, however, he'd look like any young American man. There would be nothing to outwardly imply that he is among the most well-trained and lethal warriors in history.

I'm about to ask Bacon another question, the one I really want to ask. But, before I get the words out, there's the roar of afterburners and the whole room shakes as another jet launches. Bacon smiles, points his eyes to the ceiling, and patiently waits for the noise to subside and for me to continue.

The thud of the catapult, the roar of take-off. Then quiet. It's my cue.

"Okay," I say, "let's keep going."

Bacon leans forward, whether feigning interest or being genuinely polite, I can't tell. I imagine talking to a journalist is not on his list of most desirable activities in between combat missions. It wouldn't have been for me. But he deals with it in an exceedingly polished way.

"You've seen the ISIS snuff videos," I go on. "How they burned alive the Jordanian F-16 pilot, and how they've beheaded foreign journalists."

Bacon nods.

"Does the brutality of ISIS affect you?" I ask. "Does it make it easier to kill?"

I ask the question cautiously, almost embarrassed at the words. I'm worried that my budding civilian perspective is overdramatizing the war in the way civilians are so prone to do. War becomes much less romantic, or epic, when you're in the arena every day, away from your family and friends for months on end—not for a few days or weeks at a time as us journalists typically are when we embed.

I assume that for these aviators, who have endured years of intense training to be where they are, the war is a daily task to be executed cleanly and professionally, without much thought devoted to its overall moral justice. Surely, I think, pilots like Bacon have achieved a requisite degree of mental detachment from the killing they do.

I was wrong.

At the end of my question, without a moment's pause to craft a response, as if he had thought of his reply long before I had ever asked the question, Bacon answers, "After Sinjar, their actions justified our response."

I thought back to the killing fields I'd seen in Sinjar. That atrocity was one of the key events that spurred the U.S. to begin airstrikes against ISIS. Foley's murder was another.

Bacon's words are measured and low-key as he talks about the barbarism of ISIS. No machismo or posturing. And certainly no canned responses dictated by the brass. Only a blunt declaration that hints at what lies inside the warrior's mind.

"I'll happily take the fight to the enemy, rather than them taking the fight to us," Bacon says. "That's mission accomplished."

* * *

Emotional compartmentalization is an essential skill for the military aviator. The high-stress environment of combat aviation leaves little time to reflect on its life-or-death consequences.

It can be the same with landing, especially on a carrier. The task at hand requires so much focus and is so reliant on habit patterns ingrained through years of training that the brain goes into triage, discarding sensory inputs not immediately necessary to the task at hand. That's why the landing gear handle is shaped like a wheel, blinks red, and blares an audible warning when it's time to lower the wheels. Smells, sounds, even your peripheral vision can incrementally shut down as you tap into every available neuron in a high-stress situation.

Emotions switch off, too.

Short story: When shit hits the fan, you're too busy to be scared.

Before my lunch with Bacon, I visit the squadron briefing room for Strike Fighter Squadron 87 (VFA-87), an F/A-18 Super Hornet squadron deployed on the *George H.W. Bush*.

Inside the squadron room, in which rows of leather, La-Z-Boy-style chairs are arranged like a movie theater, the pilots laugh, joke, watch movies, and munch on snacks during downtime. In the briefing area, a metal bolt hangs from a string above the assigned seat of a pilot who botched a recent landing. Humor and good-natured ribbing are essential components of fighter-pilot culture. The hidden meaning behind call signs, for example, is usually related to some act of buffoonery committed by the named pilot.

If the pilots' behavior seems incongruous with the high stakes of their profession, it's because they purposefully act that way to endure a level of stress most humans could never tolerate. The joking, the cool demeanor, the sterile vocabulary—to an outside observer those things might seem like the collective symptoms of emotional indifference. But it's all part of a well-honed culture among combat aviators, which ingrains in them the necessary mental resilience to deal with the crushing stresses of combat aviation.

"We call it compartmentalization," says Lt. Cmdr. Scott Welles, call sign "Butters," an F/A-18 Hornet pilot. "It's mentally tough."

By its very nature, combat aviation is removed from the tragedy and carnage of the battlefield. Today, as it was for the American fighter pilots who first saw combat over the World War I trenches in France a century ago, US military aviators—both the pilots and weapons systems operators—live between missions in relative safety distant from the front lines. They're physically removed from the battlefield, but they're not insulated from the moral imperative of their actions, nor are they emotionless automatons blindly executing orders.

"Does Islamic State's brutality give your mission an added sense of purpose? Does it make it easier to kill?" I ask Lt. Brandon Rogers, an F/A-18 Super Hornet pilot who goes by the call sign "Barf."

"Yeah," he replies, "the whole purpose is to protect those who can't protect themselves. Every single mission that you go on, you realize that it's one step closer to protecting our way of life."

Rogers joined the Navy in the wake of the September 11, 2001, terrorist attack and is on his fifth overall deployment—the fourth in support of combat operations.

He, too, has a deployment mustache in the works.

As is my habit, I ask, "How do you define success?"

Roger nods politely and then says flatly, "A reduction in ISIS numbers."

In May 2015, ISIS released a list of the names and addresses of about 100 US military pilots. For many, the "pilot's list," as it's known, made the war personal.

"You have an organization that's made threats against Americans and their families," says Capt. James A. McCall, commander of Carrier Air Wing Eight on the *George H. W. Bush*. "It's that kind of indiscriminate violence that brought us here. And that's incompatible with the American way of life, and incompatible with what I would say is civilized life around the world. That's why we're here."

Commensurate with his rank, McCall's answers to my questions are articulate, measured and to the point. Yet, when the "pilot's list" comes up, his true emotions surface.

"What I've learned is that I wouldn't pick on America," McCall says. "Because we're gonna come find you. And I think that's independent of politics, administrations. I think that's our American nature. If you threaten our families, our way of life, then we'll go to no end to ensure that's not going to happen."

*　　*　　*

The USS *George H. W. Bush* aircraft carrier is a veritable city at sea. It towers 20 stories above the waterline, displaces about 97,000 tons, and the flight deck comprises four and a half acres. Roughly 5,000 sailors are on board, along with 80 aircraft.

To an outside observer, flight-deck operations look like chaos. But, truly, it is an unparalleled display of teamwork, efficiency, and measured professionalism in performing "the most dangerous job in the world."

For a newbie to the flight deck like myself, you feel totally overwhelmed. It's all too easy to step in front of a moving aircraft, or get sucked into a jet engine. I'm not too proud to admit that it took a few well-timed tugs on my elbow by crew members to avoid a misstep, or disaster.

Launches are awesome, especially at night.

It's loud and confusing on the flight deck as the Hornets and Growlers advance one by one to the catapults. There, the planes stop, and the green-shirted deck crew attach the catapult shuttle to the front landing gear. The blast deflectors are raised. A few checks; some hand signals. The green-shirt runs away from beneath the landing gear to get clear and gives a thumbs-up. Now, the engines spool up to full power. The pilot scans the flight instruments and engine readings. All good. The twin afterburners illuminate like giant blowtorches as the aircraft settles into its landing-gear struts against the shackled thrust of the engines. You feel the sound in your chest, it's so loud. The pilot salutes, then braces for the squeezing G-forces of launch. The yellow-shirted "shooter" lunges like an attacking fencer, the signal for launch. One second, maybe two later, the warplane lurches forward with the initial kick of the catapult and then accelerates straight and smooth to reach 184 miles per hour in just two seconds before rocketing off the edge of the flight deck. The airborne jet slides straight away, maintaining the level of the deck for a beat before it climbs with the afterburners' fire glowing behind. As the jet flies away and the noise fades you realize you're laughing like a little kid on a roller coaster.

Then, the whole process repeats itself, again and again, until the catapults clear out and it's time for the landings. At a steady rhythm the returning jets fly over the carrier in formation before they break into the traffic pattern. When each jet lines up aft of the carrier, it seems to just hang, suspended in space as it edges toward the flight deck. The steepness of final approach becomes clear as the jet nears. And then, as if the last few moments are in fast forward, the warplane is upon the ship. It cuts down fast and lands hard. The pilot goes full throttle to have enough thrust available to take off again if the tailhook fails to catch the arresting wires.

You stand behind a painted line at the edge of the landing area. Every time a plane lands it seems like it will roll right into where you are. A tingle down the spine tells you you're in the wrong spot. The jet can't possibly stop in so short a distance—can it? But the tailhook catches, and the plane decelerates from 155 miles per hour to a full stop in about 320 feet. Free of the arresting wire, the jet's wings fold up as it taxies free of the landing area. The next plane on approach comes into focus behind the ship. Again, it looks impossible. Again, it all happens as it's supposed to.

There are subtle clues that this is a ship at war. Some warplanes coming back to land are missing a bomb or two from their wing pylons. And almost all the jets are adorned with a few rows of small bomb symbols painted beneath the canopy rails, a testament to the combat pedigree of each aircraft. These pilots and the warplanes they wield are the leading edge of America's ongoing air war against ISIS. And they kill the enemy every day.

*   *   *

Back in the mess room, as Bacon and I wrap up our interview and shake hands goodbye, I tell him something personal, which I told all the pilots during my short stint aboard the *George H.W. Bush*.

I recount the story of that evening on the rooftop of the Kurdish *peshmerga* fort outside Mosul. I tell Bacon how, when we heard the sound of American warplanes overhead, the old general had turned to me and said, "That's the sound of God."

"Damn, I've got goose bumps," Bacon says after my story. But the look on his face says more. A big smile curls that red mustache from end to end.

"You're making a difference," I tell the pilot. "You've saved a lot of lives, and America has friends forever for what you've done."

"That's awesome to hear," Bacon replies, the light reflecting off his eyes a little differently now. "Really awesome to hear."

Apathy

Throughout my time on the front lines of our country's wars, both as a combatant and as a journalist, I've heard a common, troubling refrain among America's military personnel.

Their general impression is that most people back home have either forgotten about or become apathetic to the fact that we still have soldiers deployed in combat zones around the world. This perception of indifference has entrenched an already growing divide between military and civilian societies in America.

White House chief of staff John Kelly, a retired Marine general, evoked that sentiment during a solemn press conference on October 19, 2017, following the combat deaths of four US Army soldiers in Niger.

"We don't look down upon those of you who haven't served," said Kelly, whose son, 2nd Lt. Robert Kelly, died in combat in 2010 in Afghanistan. "In fact, in a way, we're a little bit sorry because you'll never have experienced the wonderful joy you get in your heart when you do the kind of things our servicemen and women do. Not for any other reason than they love this country."

Kelly's right—even for those journalists who have been in combat. Because combat feels a lot different when you're not just worried about your own life, or getting a good story. It's a lot different when your actions decide the fate of your comrades in arms, as well as whether innocent civilians caught in harm's way will live or die.

The deaths of those four soldiers in Niger exposed America's entrenched civilian–military divide, as well as the contemporary reluctance of some media outlets to dutifully cover American combat operations unless there is a more "newsworthy" hook to the story.

Some journalists acted like the deaths in Niger illuminated some sort of shadow war going on. The truth is, then-President Barack Obama sent US troops to Niger in 2013—and it was never a secret. It just didn't make the headlines. The story had simply disappeared, like many others related to our military's combat missions, into the unending maelstrom of the modern news cycle.

Media outlets that have their priorities straight should prioritize stories not by the amount of page views, likes, or retweets they generate, but by their ultimate importance to our civil discourse. Sadly, however, that's not typically the case.

It took the deaths of four soldiers and a political feud to make US military operations in Niger newsworthy. It shouldn't be that way. But it is.

Yet, call me idealistic, but I still think my new profession is equally as important as my old one. Journalists, after all, have a unique and solemn duty to perform in a democratic republic that fields an all-volunteer military force.

The limited participation of the American population in the armed forces, the physical remoteness of the battlefields, and the technological advances in war fighting technology have made war largely an abstract burden to the overwhelming majority of Americans. Therefore, it's the responsibility of journalists to make the cost of war real and relevant to people's lives. We have to make war personal.

We have to educate citizens about the costs of war to maintain societal hesitations to the application of deadly force. And we must hold our leaders to account by demanding that they thoughtfully and wisely make the case for war when it is just and necessary—without resorting to populism or warmongering.

Educated citizens aren't so easily hoodwinked into simplistic, reductive visions of the threats facing their nation, or the reasons for their misfortunes. That's why good journalism matters.

*　　*　　*

The volunteer fighting force represents less than 1 percent of the total US population. Consequently, the trauma and sacrifice of combat is shouldered by only a small, select slice of our country. And only a small minority of Americans can truly relate to the experience of combat. Less than 8 percent of the US population has ever served in the armed forces and only 1 in 5 members of the US House and Senate is a veteran, compared with 3 out of every 4 in 1969.

The overwhelming majority of Americans are quarantined from the real-life consequences of war. Former Defense Secretary Robert Gates summed it up well when he said: "Whatever their fond sentiments for men and women in uniform, for most Americans the wars remain an abstraction. A distant and unpleasant series of news items that do not affect them personally."

When the troops return we dutifully call them heroes. Some old vets might give them a handshake and a few candy bars when they step off the plane on their return. That's how it was for me when I got back from my first combat deployment to Afghanistan.

I arrived at Baltimore-Washington International Airport late at night. The arrival hall was almost empty, except for some janitors polishing the floor with an electric floor buffer, and a group of about two dozen Vietnam War veterans handing out paper bags filled with cookies and candy bars to those of us in military uniforms streaming out from baggage claim.

One man with a gray mustache who wore a black hat that said Vietnam on it handed me a goodie bag. He then shook my hand. "Welcome home, son," he said. "We're all proud of you."

I tried hard, and unsuccessfully, not to tear up. My war had been nothing like this old man's. I spent it in the relative sanctuary of the cockpit where the enemy was usually nothing more to me than glowing black-and-white amoebas on a digital screen.

I wanted to tell that Vietnam veteran that he was the real hero; he had endured a very different kind of war and had come home to a much less appreciative nation. But all I could muster at that time was a lame, "Thanks a lot. It feels good to be home."

The old man smiled at me, then patted me on the shoulder. And that was it. A week later, I was back at work preparing for my next deployment.

To be clear, the overwhelming majority of troops and veterans—myself included—don't want special treatment, and they don't want your praise. In fact, sometimes all the "thank you for your service" comments, while well intentioned, can make a soldier feel uncomfortable. At the back of his or her mind are the constant memories of friends who made a much greater sacrifice, making us feel unworthy of the accolades.

Still, the offers of thanks do send an important message—that the soldier, sailor, airman, or Marine hasn't been forgotten. And that's more important than anything else.

All our troops and vets want is for people to pay attention. Many don't really care what you say, or how you say it. They just want to feel like the country hasn't forgotten about them, or their friends. They want to feel like their sacrifices were worth it. That the unrecoverable currency of their youths went toward a just and noble cause that, in the end, made our country and the world a little safer.

* * *

When I began a graduate journalism program at Northwestern University in 2011, just months after I had left the Air Force, I couldn't believe how unfamiliar many of my classmates were with military issues and the ongoing wars.

One student asked me if I had "caught" post-traumatic stress disorder. Like it was the flu. Some of my cohort couldn't even locate Iraq or Afghanistan on a map. And these were graduate students at one of the most prestigious journalism programs in the country—they were the cream of the crop.

My time at Northwestern as a 29-year-old was my first taste of civilian life as an adult. Once out of the bubble of military life, I was shocked to learn how the wars in Iraq and Afghanistan, which had consumed a decade of my life, had been practically forgotten by the rest of the country.

And that feeling hit a tipping point for me when my brother deployed to Afghanistan in 2013. In the days leading up to Drew's deployment and while he was downrange, I remember feeling so frustrated, bitter even, about seeing life going on uninterrupted around me back in America. It was like I wanted to grab everyone by the collar, look them in the eye, and say, "My brother is in a war. Why don't you care?"

* * *

In September 2015 I visited a US Air Force A-10 "Warthog" attack squadron stationed at an undisclosed location in the Middle East. Unexpectedly, I ran into two old friends of mine. I had gone through pilot training with them in Columbus, Mississippi, way back in 2007 when I was an Air Force lieutenant.

My old friends were now combat-tested A-10 pilots. Over dinner at the base's chow hall they told me about the carnage they were inflicting on ISIS every day. They used all the familiar lingo and clichéd expressions common to military aviation. But there was one word they used a lot, which seemed to stand out from the rest: "hunting."

In Afghanistan they had maintained a defensive mindset, they told me. The priority in that war was to defend US troops on the ground with close air support. But in the air war against ISIS over Iraq and Syria, the pilots described their mindset as offensive.

In addition to close air support and bombing missions, the A-10 pilots also flew air interdiction missions in which they patrolled for targets of opportunity—essentially they went out looking for enemy militants to kill. And they killed a lot. Sometimes one pilot would kill dozens of ISIS soldiers in a single mission. Often, by strafing the fleeing enemy with the A-10's 30 mm Gatling cannon.

What struck me most as I talked with my old friends in that desert chow hall was how casually and humbly they talked about the killing they did. They interwove stories about wives and children back home with macabre stories about the war.

The pilots' eyes seemed to focus on mine a half-beat longer than normal as they matter-of-factly described strafing an enemy checkpoint, or killing ISIS fighters one by one as they attempted escape. Sometimes, the pilot would lean back in his chair with eyes open wide, slowly shaking his head as he described the carnage he inflicted on the enemy.

But there was no remorse, not even the hint of it. And there was no questioning the justice of the war. The barbarity of ISIS had reinvigorated the sense of mission for many deployed troops, who might have been dismayed by the hamster-wheel wars we had been fighting in Iraq and Afghanistan.

ISIS's snuff videos gave their mission a special sense of justice and urgency, which we had all felt in those early years after 9/11, but somehow lost over time.

That same mindset echoed in the attitudes of many other US servicemen and women I've met in the intervening years. Our troops might not necessarily believe that the wars will be won anytime soon, but they all seemed to believe in what they were fighting for.

And, although those A-10 pilots had absolute faith in the justice of their cause, they also suspected people back home didn't understand the seriousness of the threats that face our nation, as well as the scale and ferocity of our military's unending operations to keep those threats at bay.

"People back home have no idea," one pilot told me. "But maybe it's better that way. Reality would scare the shit out of most people."

* * *

In February 2015, I joined a US Army Stryker convoy as it traveled 1,100 miles from Estonia, down through Latvia, Lithuania, Poland, and into the Czech Republic.

The convoy was called Operation Dragoon Ride; it was meant to show US resolve to defend NATO's eastern members from Russian aggression. Along the way, thousands of people lined the roadside waving US flags. Fathers had children on their shoulders. Young women blew kisses to the US troops. At each stop, no matter how small the village, hundreds of people gathered to meet the soldiers and get selfies with them. It made you proud to be American.

Maintaining a dominant military with a global presence is not just about national defense or international stability. Our military is also the torchbearer for our country's values, and a beacon of hope for people fighting for their freedom around the world. That's what our men and women in uniform fight for. That's what they're willing to die for.

It shouldn't take a tragedy to remind us of that.

2016–2017: The Journey Home

The Night Sky

I'd constructed a life in Ukraine separate from the war. Friends, an apartment, a daily workout routine. But I still went back to the front. A necessary hit of the drug from time to time. Like any good addict, I quite mistakenly thought I could quit by weaning myself off.

Then one day in June of 2016, almost on a whim, I bought a ticket to America. My parents were happy to see me, and, as to be expected, mortified by my time in Iraq and forays out to the edge of ISIS territory with the *peshmerga*. As for me, I was ready to come home, just not permanently. Not yet, anyway. I knew I'd be back in Ukraine after a few weeks at home, but I was thinking about a change. The truth was, the accumulated war-zone experiences were catching up with me. Especially the killing fields in Sinjar. That one stuck. At home, I was dour and gloomy. A bear to deal with, I must admit. Always argumentative and reflexively defensive to any perceived slight. My parents' enthusiasm to see me quickly wore thin because, quite honestly, I wasn't much fun to be around at that time.

I spent one week in Florida and then traveled with my parents to a new vacation home they had bought in the Bahamas. There, I passed the days with long walks on the beach. Alone. A storm in my mind.

Where do I go now?

Moving back to the US seemed almost unimaginable. For one, I couldn't afford it. But truthfully, I didn't want the adventure to end. The notion of sitting in a D.C. or New York newsroom, trolling Twitter and Facebook feeds for breaking news all day after I had spent the past several years in Ukraine, Iraq, Afghanistan, Paris, the Himalayas... it seemed impossible. I was ruined for office work.

My mom had to depart the Bahamas early, leaving my dad and me together alone for a few days. At that time, I was so consumed by the dark shadow of Iraq that I hardly spoke to him, even though we were living under the same roof.

One afternoon, I donned a pair of fins and a snorkel and swam out to a reef just offshore. The cool Atlantic water wrapped around my body as I dove to the bottom and back, again and again, reawakening an instinctive rhythm to my underwater movements that I'd learned as a boy, when I had practically lived in the water, surfing, swimming, diving. On that day, my muscles were like the different parts of an orchestra, separate, but perfectly in tune and in rhythm. The wars couldn't have been farther from my mind.

Later, I walked up the beach to where my dad sat under an umbrella, reading, with a half-drunk Kalik beer stuck in the sand by his side.

"Want to grab dinner tonight?" I asked.

My dad looked up from his book and smiled.

"I'd love to," he said.

*   *   *

We had dinner at a ramshackle little place with a wooden deck that overlooked a crescent-shaped bay lined by palm trees. The setting sun out across the water casted warm end-of-day beams of soft light onto my dad and me. We wore our sunglasses and drank Cuba Libres.

The conversation went in many directions. I asked about my dad's work and if he wanted to retire. For his part, my dad asked about my day-to-day life in Ukraine.

Do you get scared on the front lines?

Are you happy?

He also asked about my future, and I told him all I could. I was back to where I started, I explained, richer for the experiences but no closer toward leading the life I truly wanted.

My dad asked if I really wanted to spend my career in war zones. Hadn't I had enough of war? Wasn't it time to just think about being happy?

All good questions. And I didn't have any answers.

Finally, I asked my dad, "Are you proud of me?"

"Nolan, you're my hero," he replied. "But I worry. I thought I was done sending you off to war when you left the Air Force, and now this is even worse."

He paused, and we sat in silence for a moment. Then, he said at last, "I couldn't survive losing you."

I thought back to meeting Diane Foley, James's mom. I remembered how shattered she was by her son's death and how tightly she gripped my hand when she looked into my eyes and told me to be careful in Ukraine. I wouldn't do that to my parents, I told myself then. And yet, again and again I went to the front lines in Ukraine. I had seen ISIS fighters in the flesh on the battlefields of Iraq, and I had wandered solo over a Himalayan pass. I had done all these things with the sanctimonious justification that they were for "the story." To cast light on a forgotten injustice or to give voice to the muted heroism of those whose stories would never otherwise be told. There was something noble and necessary about what I had done as a journalist, I told myself. And I never doubted that. But there was a consequence to it all, too. And now I was face to face with how my selfish actions had exhausted my parents until their most common feeling for me was no longer one of affection, but of worry. I had become a burden. In my quest to do something noble for strangers I had hurt the people who loved me the most. Was there any virtue in that?

*   *   *

Back at the condo after dinner, my dad and I drank scotch and stayed up late, talking as friends do. At one point, when we were both well on our way, my dad exclaimed, "You have to see the night sky."

We stumbled down to the beach and stood on the cool white sand. There was no moon and not a light for miles. The ocean and the sky melded into a shimmering, horizonless void. The light of a trillion stars streaked overhead in the broad brushstrokes of the Milky Way. Truly, I think there were more stars over the Nangpa La. But, for altogether different reasons, this was the most beautiful night sky I had ever seen.

My dad and I stood there for a while, looking up.

"Thanks for showing me this," I said.

"You know," my dad said, "I could live here forever and be totally happy. I could leave everything else behind in a heartbeat."

"Me too," I said.

My dad did not immediately reply, but his hand on my shoulder said everything.

Thanksgiving

Marinka, Ukraine
November 2016

In the night I wake with a start to the sounds of artillery and gunfire. The shelling is loud enough and close enough to shake the walls. A stir from the body lying next to me. I look over at my brother, Drew, sleeping there, cocooned in a sleeping bag. Above our bunk, Kalashnikovs, body armor, and grenades hang from the walls beside Ukrainian flags. On the table next to us, letters from the families of Ukrainian soldiers alongside bullets and grenades. Ukrainian soldiers sleep in the room too, but I'm only aware of my brother's breathing.

There's a smell of burning wood and dust. A furnace heats this small room. We're on the top floor of an abandoned building the Ukrainian army's 92nd Mechanized Brigade has made into a fort in the embattled front-line town of Marinka.

The shelling rumbles through the brick and concrete walls. A sound of dust spilling like a waterfall while the windows creak from the cold winter wind outside. I think back to when Drew and I were boys. I imagine these are the sounds of a Florida thunderstorm, and my brother and I are sleeping in a fort constructed of pillows.

Then the hard metal snarl of a machine gun nearby. Reality.

My brother's presence (peacefully sleeping amid all this) is a jarring tether to home in a place far from it—in terms of both miles and circumstances. He's in Ukraine to deliver humanitarian aid to some of the war's internally displaced persons. I'm here for the story. I've seen this war before. But like the time I visited my brother in Afghanistan when he was a soldier, Drew's presence in this war makes it feel more real. I am no longer looking at it like a passenger watching the world stream by out the window of a train. I'm here. I'm in it.

It's the same for the Ukrainian soldiers, many of whom live only a few hours' drive from the front lines. If they wanted, some could drive home in the time between breakfast and lunch. A few have been away from their homes and families for almost three years to fight in this war. As I listen to my brother sleeping amid the background din of the war outside, I'm here completely. I understand, at least in some microscopic way, what this war must feel like for the Ukrainian soldiers fighting in it.

Earlier, my brother and I shiver as we stand on the roof of the 92nd Brigade's fort. The night is cold, windy, and clear. You can easily see the stars, as well as the tracer fire cutting across the sky, and the flashes of artillery and mortars exploding at regular intervals a few times a minute. You can feel the explosions in your feet. And the staccato, high-gain rattle of small-arms fire easily cuts through the frigid wind.

A Ukrainian soldier stands beside us. "This is a normal night," he says.

"How does the world not know about this?" my brother asks.

It has been like this in Ukraine for almost three years. The words "war in Ukraine" mean little anymore. It's a back-page story in Western newspapers. It's normal, expected, and just a drowned-out voice in the chaotic chorus of world news. "Before I left New York, I told a friend I was coming to Ukraine and that I'd be going out to the front lines," my brother says. "She replied, 'Oh, is that still going on?'"

My brother and I watch the spectacle of artillery for a while. When you see it in person, it's hard to look away. We talk little; what is there to say in such a moment? Except to periodically comment on what you see, as if you need confirmation that what you're seeing is in fact real.

Drew now lives and works in New York City. His military days, like mine, are a fading memory. Yet, just like me, he can't leave war behind. Not truly. He wants to be in this one, even if it isn't his. After all, if you have one war, you have them all.

"War doesn't seem to belong here, like it did in Afghanistan," Drew tells me. "This place feels familiar. And the war feels like a nightmare. How can this sort of thing still exist in the modern world, and in Europe? And how can so few people know about it?"

It is very cold and we will be going to bed soon. As the day ends, I reflect on how it began, and on the absurd distances one can travel in just one day. Distances that cover much more than miles.

This day begins in Kyiv. In my apartment, it's still dark out when I brew coffee and order an Uber to take Drew and me to the train station. Could we turn around? No. That old momentum is back again. I'm caught in the inescapable gravity of the war. No chance I'll reach escape velocity this time.

Then we're on the train for the six-hour trip to Kramatorsk. On the way, we munch on protein bars, listen to music on our iPhones, and read novels. The train has Wi-Fi, so we check email, too.

Arrival in Kramatorsk. We meet our driver and translator, and take possession of our body armor and helmets. Then we're on the road. Our driver takes a wrong turn and we get stuck in the mud. We get out, but the car, a black Mercedes, is broken down.

Our translator is on her cell phone in a flash, making alternate plans. I worry that this trip is quickly becoming a disaster, and we'll not even get out to the front lines. But the translator comes through and arranges another driver. Several hours later, the new driver, Edward, picks us up from the side of the road where we wait, shivering. We're on our way again. This time in a yellow van.

It's early afternoon now. But in Ukraine the winter sun sets at about 4:30 p.m. We're in a race to get to Marinka before nightfall. We zip along the potholed, two-lane roads that cut through wide-open fields, many of which are still green even in mid-November. The sun dips lower and lower, and we worry if we'll get there in time. The sky turns orange, and then fades to violet. It's almost night. We're lucky and get through the checkpoints with no hassle. Our driver is a friend of the soldiers; he often transports supplies out to the front lines. Edward has a special pass, and the soldiers wave us through without even checking our passports.

We're driving through farmland and villages, but it feels like the savage wild. Like in the Himalayas, where with the night comes the deadly cold. Or on the Serengeti, where the predators emerge after sunset. Here in eastern Ukraine, with the night comes the war.

Stars begin to spot the sky. The long, straight road cuts across an open plain. Ahead is the blacked-out silhouette of buildings in Marinka. Beyond is Donetsk, the separatist stronghold. Somewhere ahead, lurking invisibly in the fading embers of the day, is the war. Here in the car, you can't see it or hear it yet. But you can feel it, heavy on your chest, a flutter of butterflies in the stomach, a feeling of adrenaline restlessness. All products of your imagination alone. Some sixth sense, a leftover of evolution hidden deep within the primordial folds of your brain, alerts you to the danger in the night.

When we arrive in Marinka it's almost completely dark, but the artillery-blasted apartment blocks are still clearly visible. We pull up to the apartment building where we are to meet a family for dinner. Stepping out of the van, the not-too-distant "thud, thud, thud" of mortars greets us. The crackle of machine guns replies. The war. We're here.

The stairway in the apartment building is dark. We use our iPhones for flashlights. There is hardly anyone left living in the building. Half of Marinka's original 10,000 residents have left. The war sent them away. We pass through the threshold of the door, and inside the apartment the war is instantly a memory. The owner, a former Red Army helicopter maintainer, has jury-rigged his home for electricity and running water. It feels like home.

We sit down for dinner, a Kazakh meal the old veteran learned while in the Soviet military. He pours us glasses of a homemade alcohol made from walnuts. My brother and I are both Air Force veterans. Me from Afghanistan and Iraq; Drew from several times in Afghanistan. We clink glasses with this old Soviet soldier. All three of us served in Afghanistan. We know the same places, the same names. Some of the same enemies. Such different circumstances. Tonight we are friends.

The old soldier's wife brings out his Soviet uniform and points admiringly to his many medals. He pours more moonshine for all of us. Surreal is not enough of a word; we emblazon the memory as best we can.

After dinner we travel across town to where the Ukrainian soldiers are holed up. They have turned an abandoned building and its surrounding area into a fort.

Tanks and armored personnel carriers are scattered in the muddy yard and under concealment in different hiding places. We are escorted into a room where more than a dozen soldiers lounge in their bunks.

At first, silence. Trepidation as our translator explains who we are. Then, when she explains that we are both veterans of America's wars, a switch flips. Instantly, easily, the Ukrainian troops accept my brother and me in their midst.

I explain that I'm a journalist now, no longer a pilot. And I'm here to report on their war. The soldiers tell us they feel forgotten—by their own government, as well as by the world.

The Ukrainian soldiers treat my brother and me as honored guests. A bottle of something comes out. Food is passed around. Bread, *salo*, and fried potatoes. Toasts, professions of friendship. Questions about New York City, Miami, our new president-elect. They want to know about life in the American military, how much we were paid, the benefits we now get as veterans. They ask our opinions of Ukrainian women. I tell them I have a Ukrainian girlfriend. A picture comes out of my wallet. Heads nod approvingly.

We ask the Ukrainian soldiers what they're fighting for. They talk about freedom, democracy, protecting their families. My brother and I nod our heads approvingly.

Hands slapping shoulders, stories told through a mixture of sign language and the skills of our translator.

It's two days before Thanksgiving, and although the spread of food and drink is unfamiliar, the feelings are all the same. How is it possible that this place can so easily feel like home?

A few hours after sunset, we witness the cease-fire's daily charade. As is their habit, the OSCE cease-fire monitors have gone home for the night, so the war begins again in earnest. The every-so-often boom of artillery and crackle of small arms. The walls rattle from the shelling. It's not close enough to really scare you, but close enough to switch you into another mode of existing that's only possible in something like war. The Ukrainian soldiers retaliate with laughter and conversation. As if camaraderie and humor are the surest defenses against the bullets and bombs. There is something about laughing that overwrites the fear of dying.

My brother and I and a few soldiers step outside. The night air is frigid. We look at the tanks and the armored vehicles. We have a cigarette or two with the soldiers. Neither my brother nor I are smokers, but under the present circumstances it feels natural.

The soldiers say they can usually hear enemy drones orbiting overhead at night. But not on this night because the wind is too strong. Huddled together in the cold darkness, smoking, with the orchestra of war as our background din, I imagine life here is not so different than it was for the soldiers who fought over this land in World War II.

Tens of millions died in that war, while 10,000 have died in this one. Yet, it is the geographic scale of this war that makes it less deadly, not the weapons, nor the conviction of its soldiers. Despite a frequency and intensity of shooting that leaves my brother and me wide-eyed, the soldiers are dismissive. It's a "regular night," they say.

"You should be here when it's really active," one says. I can see his lips curl to a smile in the dark.

We go to the roof to watch the war for a while, and then it's time for bed. We bed down in a room with a few other soldiers. I wrap myself in blankets. Next to me is my brother in his sleeping bag. The war is outside, a steel storm that thunders all night.

In the morning, we're up early. A 22-year-old private named Vsevolod Chernetskyi comes with breakfast prepared. A mix of buckwheat and vegetables. Simple soldier fare. We make coffee, too, and drink it from tin mugs.

We sit on ammo crates and eat. Chernetskyi shows me videos from the US-made Raven drone he operates. The grainy aerial images are familiar to me. That's my war.

There's no running water, so we wash our dishes from breakfast with water from a bucket. Outside the warmth of the room in which we slept is another room where random gear, both personal and military, is scattered. Tins of food and supply parcels are stacked on a table made of plywood and cinder blocks. After almost three years of war, and despite the fact that one could drive to a grocery store from here in under an hour, the Ukrainian troops are still living in what is basically a glorified campsite.

They steal electricity from the local power grid, and draw water from a local well. The innovative soldiers who try to incorporate off-the-shelf technology onto the battlefield—like using tablets and laptops for maps instead of paper copies—have to use their own money to make those changes happen.

The military takes care of the weapons, ammunition, and the bare necessities of food and water. But civilian volunteers still bring in nearly everything else, including things like body armor and long underwear.

The engine of a Soviet armored personnel carrier called a BMP is warming up outside. The soldiers want to take my brother and me on a short patrol through no man's land in the 1970s-vintage vehicle. We agree with foolhardy enthusiasm. Shortly thereafter we're standing in two open hatches on top of the armored vehicle as we cut across the edge of open fields, up and over berms, and down and across ditches.

The BMP swings hard to the left and right as it makes turns. The engine is loud. My hands, even under gloves, go numb from the cold while holding onto the metal hatch door. Soon, our faces are covered in a film of sticky, black oil residue from the exhaust growling out of the 40-year-old Soviet engine.

Suddenly, the BMP stops, spins around, and makes a beeline back to the Ukrainian fort. There is frantic talk in Russian, but we understand nothing. My brother and I learn later that separatists had spotted us. A single armored personnel carrier alone in an open field would have been an easy target. We never understand the danger until it's over.

We laugh about it.

Three hours by car and we're back in Kramatorsk at a restaurant eating salmon fillets and borscht, and drinking beer. We clink glasses to celebrate a successful trip. Heads shaking in disbelief for what we have experienced.

Then at the train station, we stand on the platform smoking cigarettes, a habit now. We haven't left the front lines quite yet. Soldiers in uniform are among the crowd waiting to board the train.

"It feels like World War II," Drew says.

On the train we talk and listen to music and munch on chicken wings and sandwiches. It's a six-hour trip back to Kyiv. An empty, metallic feeling in your chest where the adrenaline flutters used to be. Now, you feel calm and happy and laugh about things which to an outside observer might seem crazy to laugh about. Three hours in a car and six by train is hardly enough time to leave the war behind. It stays inside of you.

Back in Kyiv we're beyond the reach of the bullets and the bombs. Walking the city streets, the war feels like a secret between my brother and me. Back to the cocktail bars, the McDonald's restaurants, and Niketown stores. You see the world through the lens of the question: "How could things be like this with a war still going on?" It felt like that coming home from Iraq and Afghanistan, too, I remember. All wars, like the soldiers who fight in them, have much more in common than we sometimes immediately realize. Walking in Kyiv, I think: "Is this real life? Or, did we leave it behind in Marinka?"

More and more, it feels like the only true thing is what we experienced on the front lines. Therein lies the danger of bringing a piece of home with you. Because when the war begins to feel a little like home, you can never truly leave it. But there's something different waiting for me now in Kyiv. Something more than the mad swirl of normal life that seems so out of place, so close in time and space to the war.

Now, it feels like I'm coming home and not leaving it behind.

I open the door to my apartment and walk quietly into the bedroom where she's sleeping. I sit down beside her and kiss her on her forehead. She wakes.

"I missed you," I say.

"If not me, then who?" she replies.

Love and War

I met her and then I was in love. There was no falling for anything.

On a Saturday in September, I was at a bar talking with a friend, and then there she was. I didn't need more than one look to know. She needed our first date, which happened the next day. But she knew, too. Three months later, Lilya was living with me. One year later, we were engaged. Today, we're married.

I don't really believe in this sort of thing, but I can't help but feel as if some force—deliberate or not—intervened, fating our paths to cross. It was too perfectly constructed to have happened that way on its own, it seems to me. But, maybe it was just a coincidence. A miraculous stroke of good fortune.

I once wrote a letter to myself as an old man. In it, I said he had all the answers and I had all the questions. I wrote that letter on my 22nd birthday while I was living in Paris as a graduate student, when many things still had to happen. Now, more than a decade later, I had some of those answers. Lilly was one of them.

At home in our apartment in Kyiv. She's standing there in the kitchen, making tea. She's wearing my gray T-shirt over her thin ballerina's body. Her long dark hair is pulled back in a pony tail. She wears no make-up over her angular cheeks. Natural, beautiful. I watch her green eyes, looking for a portal into the places within. She catches me staring.

"Nolan?" she says, inflecting her voice like she has something to ask. "Yes?"

"I love you," she says.

There are, as always, worries and other things orbiting around this moment, threatening to pull me away from the here and now. But I'm barely aware of them.

I haven't gone back to the war for a while. And I don't know if I want to, anyway. Am I hiding from the war, or have I truly left it?

At the open window, now, writing these words. Clickety-clackety-click on the keyboard. A bird chirps, the breeze rustles, the trees bend. Sun shining, bright blue sky, no clouds. Spring, life, love, thoughts of futures and of the good things to come. Today, we will go for a walk. She's looking lovely. And me, feeling reborn and fresh. But the war is still there. Even when I don't go to it, even on a day like this one when the universe gives me every reason there could ever be to not spend one more moment thinking about the war. Still, I can't help it.

I hear Daniel's voice, "I want to get out of these battles. I want to forget it. But I can't."

Now I hear Lilly. She says it's time to go. Today is meant for something else. The day beckons, my fingers type furiously to get these words down before I can't stand it any longer. I want to be out there, with her, among life's beautiful things. A part of the world, not an observer of it. Today, I'll take a holiday from the war. First, I write:

Love and war are one and one and nothing left between the two. It's the same, you know, to want to kill or die for something. You give it all away for both, you understand. No question about that. No other way to see it through.

I had already been in my own wars. I had already lost what I had to lose, doing what I had to do. There was nothing left. Not there, no longer here. I'm alive and well and dead and gone and young and old. Understand? No? That's fine, I didn't expect you to.

I felt out of place and foreign, even in the places that should feel like home. Back in America, they say thanks and buy me a beer. But how could they understand? They've never been there.

I was skipping across the surface of life, leaving ripples to nowhere. It seemed pointless and silly and stupid and worthless and I was mad and impatient and started to wish I was back in the war just so I would give a damn again.

So that's why Ukraine, and that's why her. I can't speak the language, I don't know the songs or the dances or the names of the streets, or much about anything at all.

But I feel at home here, and with her. More than I have in a long time. I'm in a place where everyone, from the man serving my beer to the girl whose lips I want to kiss, they all understand me because they are me. They want another tomorrow more than a lifetime of todays. We live and love and laugh and cry and worry and are sad and angry and hopeful and scared.

We are all the things you can only be if tomorrow is a silly dream that you try for anyway, even if it kills you.

Maybe that's why love and war twist and tangle the way they do.

Those two things have the power to erase yesterday and make you happy and fearless about tomorrow. To find a person, or a cause, that is more important than you is the highest thing a soul can do, after all. And once you have done one you can do the other with ease.

That's why warriors fight harder and love harder than anyone else.

That's why I love Ukraine, and her. It's because I'm alive here. And I want to live so damn bad, you can't know.

Escape Velocity

Lilly and I celebrated our first Christmas together in December 2016. We bought a small tree and decorated it for when my parents came to visit—it was their first time in Ukraine during the more than two years I had so far been living there.

Together, the four of us went to the ballet and to my favorite cafés and restaurants. I took them to the memorial at the place where the snipers had shot the protesters during the 2014 revolution, where there are still bullet holes in the trees and in light poles. We walked along

Khreshchatyk and down St. Andrew's Descent. I took them to all the places that had been the backdrop to those past few years of my life. And, of course, my parents met Lilly. My future.

"You are a wonder," my mom told me. "I'm so proud of the man you've become." The happiness in her eyes was clear.

That Christmas, more than any other, was a vivid reminder of how much my life had changed. The year prior, I was home in America for the holiday. Lonely, and lost, fresh from trips that fall and winter to Iraq, the Himalayas. I felt like I was caught in the inescapable gravity of war, doomed to never break free.

One year later, everything had changed. I felt, for the first time in a long while, that I had truly advanced toward a life that might make me happy.

It was wonderful to have my parents there with me in Kyiv and with Lilly. And then, in a flash it seemed, the holidays were over, my parents were gone and it was back to living and working. The months slid by. I went to the war a time or two as winter faded into spring. Once, a mortar narrowly missed me on a visit to the trenches outside the front-line town of Avdiivka. The explosion was so close that it left my ears ringing for days. Yet, unlike in trips past, there was no high from that close brush with death. Only a feeling of stupidity and regret for having risked the life ahead with Lilly for one more taste of war.

After that trip, I made a promise to Lilly that I wouldn't go back to the front lines anymore. I wasn't willing to trade a lifetime with her for a hit of that old drug. And I hated how she worried about me.

In spring, we visited Lilly's parents in her native town of Komsomolsk. On the train ride back to Kyiv, we stretched out on the top two bunks in a four-person sleeper berth. It was night and the lights outside streamed by like spotlight beams through the small gap in between the flimsy curtains over the window. Barely enough light to see Lilly staring at me. I thought she might be crying, but I couldn't tell in the flashes of half-light.

"Is everything okay?" I asked.

We had just been talking about an offer I had received to go back to Afghanistan for a few weeks to embed with US Special Forces. I wasn't sure if I wanted to do it. She wasn't going to tell me what to do, one way or the other, but I knew she didn't want me to go.

"Lilly?" I asked again.

Still, she was silent.

"If I lost you…" she said at last, hesitating again. "It would destroy me. My whole life would be ruined."

I didn't tell her right then, but I had made up my mind. I wasn't going.

Funny. It had once been such an obsession of mine to get back to war. I had yearned for it like I had been holding my breath and the war was my oxygen. Now, it was so easy to give up war for the sake of happiness with Lilly.

It wasn't even a choice, really.

I had finally reached escape velocity.

For a long time, I've felt like I was in search of something. A new career. A new home. Maybe, a new sense of purpose after the military. That search led me to the ends of the earth, and into more than a few dangerous circumstances.

In the summer of 2014, I had a one-way plane ticket to Ukraine. I left to report on the war, thinking I'd only be gone for about two weeks. Now, looking back all these years later, I know there was only one path I was ever supposed to take. It was that one-way ticket to Ukraine, which led to Lilly. And that path to her was the way back home for which I'd always been searching. Home, as I've learned, has nothing to do with geography.

One of my favorite quotes is from Steve Jobs. At the end of his life, as he was dying from cancer, Jobs said, "In life, you can't connect the dots looking forward; you can only connect them looking backwards. So you have to trust that the dots will somehow connect in your future…"

Instead of me going back to Afghanistan, Lilly and I are planning our life together. Maybe, her love was what had always been missing.

With my wife, Lilly, in Greece. I promised her that I'd stop going to the front lines—and I've never regretted it.

Now, with her at my side, I have finally rediscovered the promise and the wonder that I felt as a 16-year-old, setting off for the Himalayas. I felt the same way when I saw Lilly for the first time. That feeling, as on the first day in a new country, when everything is new and unexplored and there are so many more questions than answers.

In the end, that's what I need more than war.